Sabine Hönig / Ursula Kutschera

*Aroma*kitchen

COOKING WITH ESSENTIAL OILS

Schiffer Publishing Ltd

4880 Lower Valley Road · Atglen, PA 19310

Contents

Introduction

Eliane Zimmermann

I am truly lucky, as my dreams are still being fulfilled. However, my desire for a cookbook with recipes that can be prepared in little time and that include fantastic, healthy essential oils did not come to fruition for a long time. In my workshops and seminars I kept encouraging participants to compile recipes for delicious dishes. A few small booklets and various pamphlets were the result. Because cooking without essential oils is like cooking without salt for me, I started to put together a collection of aroma kitchen recipes with tantalizing photos. However, none of this found its way into the kitchen of the many fans of varied and healthy nutrition. Until now.

Essential oils have been used for cooking only since the mid-1980s. It happened as a consequence of the catastrophe at Chernobyl, when a Munich couple had to find a solution: Maria and Thomas Kettenring couldn´t prepare their vegetarian dishes with fresh herbs and spices because the radioactivity of many of the ingredients was too high.

At the same time the two passionate cooks and nutritional professionals were looking for alternatives to the increasingly synthetic flavoring of food. They were already involved in one of the first German essential oil companies. They realized that the commercially available essential oils and herbs were not affected by the radioactivity. It was fairly obvious that they should start cooking with them!

Because essential oils consist of highly concentrated herb and spice extracts, much experimentation was necessary to find out how to provide both a refined taste and nutritional value to the seasoned dishes. It wasn´t as simple as adding a drop of cinnamon, basil, or ginger oil to the food! Many dishes would be over-spiced or even worse. Trial and error has yielded many wonderful recipes. The result was the first German-language aroma cookbook, which was published in several expanded editions. Even well-known chefs are now dedicated to this "art of aroma." But while the industrial flavoring of food is still advancing and is not limited by legislation, users and manufacturers of natural essential oils are confronted with increasing regulations and limitations.

Spicing with plants that are rich in natural aromas is certainly as old as humanity itself. From the time when our ancestors were walking on all fours, delicately scented molecules showed the way to healthy and wholesome food. All the creatures who walk upright intuitively know through their noses whether a foodstuff is spoiled or not. But over time, those aromas have been masked and colorful packaging with in-your-face advertising has replaced this valuable "antenna" on our faces. Homo sapiens are on the way to forgetting their capacity to distinguish good from bad. Useless fillings and food ingredients, allergy-provoking substances, hyperactivating hormone-like substances, Alzheimer-inducing sweeteners, and rainbow-like food coloring have led to the taste buds unlearning and even forgetting previous abilities.

This olfactory devolution might even contribute to dementia, as the minute sensory region of the brain atrophies during the early stages of the disease, the region which processes both memory and the sense of smell, the hippocampus. It is possible that tumors are facilitated because of the lack of subtle pheromones that plants use to call pollinating insects, which in turn combat enemies which feed on the plants. In recent years, there have been numerous scientific papers that have shown that many ingredients of essential oils can protect against malignant tumors. Even existing cancers

have been contained in animal experiments, including the inhibition by some essential oils of the creation of blood vessels that provide nutrition to the cancerous cells.

So it is about time for a recipe book that shows how easy it is to eat in a healthy and delicious way. No "haute cuisine," but everyday delicacies that can be prepared in no time. From salad dressings to peppy drinks, there is nothing in the realm of aroma cooking that cannot be improved with natural essential oils, both to boost your health and satisfy your demanding sense of taste. I only wish that this book reaches a very wide audience!

Eliane Zimmermann

Preface

Cooking has always been our passion. When we started to delve into the fascinating world of essential oils years ago, it was only natural for us to use these wonderful essences in our kitchen as well. For us, cooking is a very creative activity. Utilizing essential oils leaves a lot of room to try out new things and to experiment in the kitchen with unique aromas.

Adding aroma to dishes with essential oils is more "spicing" than "perfuming," because the taste sensation is based on the smell rather than the palate. The fact is that the human tongue and palate know only five tastes. Our nose complements this rather limited sense of taste. Much of what we think we taste is actually derived via the sense of smell. Because the nose and the mouth are connected, taste and smell complement each other. And whoever has had a cold knows that without the sense of smell, the food simply does not taste good.

Both of us had the idea to create a cookbook independently. We had started to incorporate essential oils into our recipes. We both discovered that there was little if anything about this to be found in books. Indications for the amounts of the essential oils or recipes with essential oils were a mere fantasy! So we both thought: I will write a cookbook. We were lucky to run into each other before publishing two books about the subject. We united our inspirations, our networks, and our ideas, and decided to write the book together. It was the right decision—we had much fun while "working" on this book. Both of us contributed our experience and we motivated each other, as the road to the finished book seemed to be almost endless.

By the way, we are normal, everyday women, not trained cooks. We simply love good food and pursue our independent occupations. We might be a little "old-school" because we actually cook every day with fresh ingredients and use as few instant and processed products as possible to nourish our loved ones in a healthy and varied way.

The recipes in this book are not sophistries of the haute cuisine that only kitchen professionals are able to create. We want to show you that everyone can create everyday dishes that are easy to prepare and can be refined with some "essential" help.

We hope that you have lots of fun while recreating these dishes! And please allow yourself to experiment...

Sabine Hönig
Ursula Kutschera

Acknowledgments

The fact that you are holding this cookbook in your hands now is due not only to our passion for cooking and our tenacity while working on this common project. More than anything, this book was possible because many of our many dear friends believed in our ability as authors and contributed with their knowledge and special talents.

We want to thank particularly our husbands, who played the role of brave and critical tasters of our dishes and who tolerated the fact that, for a long time, the only thing we had on our minds was essential oils and cooking!

A heartfelt thanks goes to those who have assisted us with their knowledge, as well as all kinds of issues around writing, editorial topics, marketing, and factual information about foodstuffs and cooking. Our special thanks to those friends and acquaintances who have volunteered as cooks. Their feedback has proven that these dishes can be prepared by both experienced and novice cooks without any problem.

Our thanks goes also to our sponsors who have supported us and who have trusted in the success of this cookbook.

Theoretical
information about essential oils

The character of essential oils

Every plant develops its life force over the course of the four seasons. It follows the changing temperature in a harmonic way and grows roots, leaves, flowers, and fruits. Depending on the plant species it also develops aromatic particles in its secondary metabolism—essential oils—which serve these functions for the plant:

- communication
- medicines
- pest repellents
- attraction for pollinating insects

Depending on the climatic conditions, location, and kind of soil, the plant of a certain genus develops different chemotypes (e.g., thyme ct. linalool, ct. thymol). These chemotypes are different in their effect, as well as in their smell and taste.

Essential oils should not be confused with plant oils as such. Plant oils have a limited storage period as they may become rancid when in contact with oxygen. The plant oils are used among other things as basic oils for massage and body oils, as nurturing ingredients for cosmetics, and to create spice items for the kitchen.

Essential oils are found in several different parts of the plant material:

- in the blossoms (e.g., jasmine, rose, chamomile, mimosa)
- in the leaves (e.g., sage, rosemary, melissa)
- in the roots (e.g., vetiver)
- in the fruit (e.g., cilantro, caraway)
- in the wood (e.g., cedarwood, sandalwood, tulipwood)
- in the bark (e.g., cinnamon bark)
- in the resin (e.g., frankincense, styrax, myrrh)
- in the fruit peel (e.g., all citrus fruits).

Some plants produce essential oils in several parts. Such is the case with the orange tree, of which three essential oils can be manufactured:

- orange peel oil
- orange leave oil (petitgrain)
- orange flower oil (neroli).

Depending on the type of plant or the part of the plant, their essential oils can be quite different in color and consistency. For example, citrus oils are often the color of the peel from which they were derived—orange to light yellow. Essential oils derived from resin or roots are often thick and heavy and need to be removed from the bottle with small spatulas (e.g., vetiver or styrax).

The production of essential oils

There are different methods to produce the aromatic essences. They not only contain the plant's essence but its biochemical constituents, which are used both in phytotherapy and aroma therapy. Many of these plant extracts have been critical in the production of modern medicines.

The method and the required plant mass are different for every oil. You need about 880 pounds of sandalwood to produce 2 pounds of sandalwood oil, and some 80 to 100

hours. To distill one pound of rose oil you need about two-and-a-half tons of rose flowers! However, for one pound of lemon oil, only 100 pounds of fruit peel are needed. This explains why some essential oils are very valuable and costly. They are simply "natural gold"!

Water vapor distillation
This method is the most common way of producing essential oils and is used for most plants. It is similar to distilling alcohol. Care must be taken, however, to keep the temperature and pressure as low as possible, so as not to break up the chemical bonds. The plant matter is placed in a sieve over hot water. The hot vapor releases the essential oils and they rise with the vapor. As the vapor cool, the essential oils and water condense and are collected in the distilling cooler. Since essential oils are usually lighter than water and are not water-soluble, they can be removed from the surface of the water. The remaining water is called hydrolate.

Pressure extraction
To produce citrus oils, the peel of the fruit is pressed until the oil cells burst open and release the essential oil. The essential oil is soaked up with sponges which are then squeezed again. Today, this method is not very common and is usually replaced by the less elaborate expression method described below.

Expression
Several steps are necessary to extract essential oils from peels by the delicate method of expression. First, the peels are washed and rasped in the presence of water on peeling drums. The result is an emulsion of essential oil, water, and solid material, which is then centrifuged to produce the pure essential oil.

Theoretical Information about Essential Oils

Enfleurage

This method extracts essential oils from flowers by placing them on boards that are covered with animal fat. The fat removes the essential oils from the flowers. Then the boards are cleaned with alcohol. Pure flower oil is produced this way (absolute d'enfleurage). Due to its very high cost this production method is rarely used today.

Solvent extraction

For plants which cannot be distilled, solvents such as hexane and alcohol are used to dissolve the essential oil contained in the plant. The solvent is then removed with vacuum distillation. The filtering process then removes the essential oil from the plant matter, as well as the resulting wax.

CO_2-extraction

This relatively new production method allows us to capture the oils of plants for which there was no previous method (e.g., coffee, hops). It uses carbon dioxide, which dissolves non-polar elements, and is used to extract natural compounds like essential oils. With a relatively high pressure and at temperatures around 90° Fahrenheit or lower, the essential oils are dissolved. Carbon dioxide as a solvent results in essential oils being completely uncontaminated, since CO_2 evaporates under normal atmospheric pressures. The resulting essential oils are almost identical to the original plant. However, this is a very expensive method. It is interesting to note that this method conserves any spicy-hot compounds in the essential oil. This means that some of the oils produced via this method (e.g., ginger or pepper oil) are very hot and need to be used very carefully.

Synthetic imitation

Cheap industrial aromas are usually produced by imitation, utilizing petroleum. The identity (biochemical properties and aroma) can be recreated in the laboratory to about 80%. This method is cheaper, but there are 20% of the natural ingredients missing, which changes the overall character of the essential oil. They are not used in aroma treatments and applications because their biochemical effects are drastically altered or absent.

Quality considerations

The supply of essential oils is almost impossible to gauge. There are many oils at very low prices. They are not suitable for the aroma kitchen! We would like to provide some guidance so you can tell good essential oils from bad ones. Check that all of your essential oils are 100% natural and pure, and preferably from natural organic production. The natural origin of citrus oils is particularly important. Some oils are produced from the peels of citrus fruit, which often contain pesticides. Also, the peel of citrus fruit is often treated with wax. These compounds can reach the final product during the extraction of the essential oils. Only buy essential oils where you can get comprehensive consultation and information. However, quality has its price. The quality of essential oils depends on the plant quality and the distillation procedure and method.

Plant quality

Look for pesticide-free cultivation, a known plant species, harvesting at optimal maturity, and a confirmed chemotype (see page 9).

Distillation

It is important to allow sufficient time during distillation to get all of the components. Low-pressure distillation without additional extraction compounds works best.

Essential oil quality
- No contamination with synthetic molecules
- No extraction of individual compounds via distillation
- No eliminated terpenes
- No over-oxidization

Reduced quality may be due to
- Dilution with
  - fatty oils
  - alcohol
  - cheap essential oils
- standardization (removing compounds)
- wrong labeling
- use of emulsifiers
- synthetic treatment

The following minimum labeling information should give you a certain sense of assurance that the essential oils are of good quality:

1. 100 % natural essential oil
2. English plant name
3. botanical plant name (chemotype)
4. utilized part of plant
5. production method
6. country of origin of plant
7. lot number
8. shelf life
9. depending on the declared use, either
   - hazard labeling (e.g., skull and crossbones when used for room aromatization and/or for aroma therapy
   - potentially allergenic compounds and a recommendation for cosmetic application when intended for aroma therapy usage

Bottling
The oils must always be bottled in dark bottles. Generally, the more information you have apart from the above indications (e.g., method of planting and additional certified qualities like organic production, etc.) the better your source.

Good providers may be able to provide certified organic production and quality certificates.

Price
Price is also an indication of good quality. Here are some guidelines:
- 10 ml lavender extract (Lavandula angustifolia) about $20
- 10 ml orange oil (Citrus sinensis) about $10
- 1 ml Bulgarian rose oil about $40
- 1 ml melissa (Melissa officinalis) about $30

Organically produced oils are between $5 to $10 more expensive. Essential oils are particularly good if they originate from the normal growing regions of the plants, e.g., orange oil from Sicily or lavender oil from France. Usually these oils are a little more expensive, but they are often more refined as to their aroma and sometimes contain more biochemical compounds.

Dilution
Very expensive and intense essential oils like rose, melissa, or neroli are often diluted with jojoba oil for better dosage. This is not a problem and does not constitute a lower quality as long as this fact and the grade of dilution is stated on the bottle. Jojoba oil has a conservation effect when mixed with essential oils. However, oils diluted with jojoba oil are not suitable for the aroma kitchen. For this purpose, you should use pure oil which is sold in 1 ml units.

Usage and effects outside of the aroma kitchen

Essential oils are not only a great addition for the aroma kitchen. Due to their varied range of effects they are also used in aroma cosmetics, for massages, for room aromatization, and aroma therapy.

So here is a little excursion into the world of essential oils and their application outside of the kitchen in order to show all you can do with these aromatic essences.

Effect

Essential oils work on two levels. Via our sense of smell they have a direct influence on our emotions and can generate positive, concentration-facilitating, brighter, or more relaxing sensations. The biochemical plant compounds react with the physical body.

Natural essential oils are composed of a large number of different biochemical compounds. It is not only each compound by itself, but the combined effect of all of them that produces a specific effect. For example, essential oils can be disinfecting, antiseptic and antiviral, pain-relieving, anti-inflammatory, good for the skin, and immune system-boosting.

Application

Apart from their excellent quality (see "Quality considerations") it is important to know about the active compounds, their effect, and possible precautions (also see the chart of the most popular essential oils of the aroma kitchen, page 22 and

following). Because of their high concentration, essential oils must be used sparingly and with care. When aroma therapy is applied with knowledge and the right dosage, it is suitable for people of all ages. Aroma therapy is understood to be the application of 100% natural essential oils to maintain and to improve the physical, mental, and spiritual wellbeing. Essential oils are applied via the sense of smell, the skin, or the mucous membranes.

The sense of smell

Room fragrancing

One of the most well-known uses of essential oils is room fragrancing. The high cultures of antiquity used oils to cleanse rooms spiritually with incense and aromatic essences. The distillation technique was known in Europe since the tenth century and essential oils for room fragrancing became an important factor. Aroma lamps, aroma streamers, and diffusors are used for room fragrancing with essential oils.

When using aroma lamps with tea light candles, you need to consider the size of the evaporator bowl. If it is too small, the water may evaporate too quickly and the essential oil will get burned. The distance between the candle and the evaporator bowl should be at least four inches. The number of drops depends on the size of the room to be fragranced and the intensity of the oil. If the room is no larger than 300 square feet you will need 4–10 drops of oil. Lively and fresh aromas such as citrus evaporate quickly, while flowery and earthy aromas can still be noticed after many hours. Bedrooms, children´s rooms, and hospital rooms and geriatric institutions are not suitable for the use of fragrance lamps with an open flame. In these cases, the electric version or a diffusor are preferable.

Room fragrancing should not be done continuously but in intervals. After a 20-minute fragrancing session with 100% pure essential oils, wait several hours before the next session, ventilating the rooms repeatedly. This assures a healthy room ambience. Longer sessions do not make sense when you spend a long time in one room, as the nose "switches off" its perception after 20 minutes to be able to notice other scents and possible danger.

Essential oils can neutralize unpleasant smells and disinfect the air. Citrus aromas are particularly suited for refreshing the air of a room, but so are the essential oils of lemongrass, litsea cubeba, or conifer woods. To disinfect the room during the flu season, you can use eucalyptus, myrtle, ginger, and lemon. Because smells enter our limbic system, our emotional center, without any filtering process, they constitute a bridge between our physical and spiritual wellbeing. If they are used correctly they can provide a special ambience to rooms and elicit moods in a controlled manner.

Fresh aromas like conifer woods, mint, lemon, grapefruit, bergamot, litsea cubea, lemongrass, palmarosa, and lavender cause rooms to seem larger. But aromas like patchouli, styrax, oak moss, heavy floral scents, cinnamon, clove, orange, cilantro, vanilla, or benzoin provide a feeling of security and warmth. Essential oils like lemon, mint, eucalyptus, and conifer woods are great to cool down rooms when it is hot. Aroma mixes work better than individual aromas. However, it is not advisable to use room fragrances when serving meals cooked with essential oils as the sense of smell might be overwhelmed.

Direct smell or dry inhalation
You may still remember this type of application from the old movies, where elegant ladies had a little bottle handy in case of too much excitement or fainting. This type of application consists of smelling the flask or putting a drop of the essential oil on a handkerchief and holding it under your nose. Orange flower oil (neroli) or real melissa (melissa officinalis) have proven to be effective in case of stressful moments or demanding situations such as exams. Both oils have a calming effect on the nerves without causing fatigue.

Application on the skin

Aroma cosmetics
Many essential oils contain components which are beneficial for the skin, such as rose flower oil, neroli and incense, lavender, ylang-ylang, or cedar. Essential oils are not only utilized because of their delicious aroma, but also because of their effects on the skin. It is easy to make great aromatic body or massage oils combining high-quality fatty plant oils with essential oils. You can also create balms, lotions, deodorants, natural perfumes, and ointments for home use.

Natural perfume

Of course, you can also create your own natural perfume from your favorite oils. Follow the basic 1-2-4 rule for mixing aromas: 1 part basic note (e.g., sandalwood, vetiver, benzoin), 2 parts heart note (e.g., flower or herb oils like rose, neroli, lavender, marjoram) and 4 parts head note (e.g., citrus oils like orange, lemon, bergamot) However, mixing perfumes requires some experience and an experienced nose, as perfumes made from essential oils change their aroma while "maturing." A lasting perfume that slowly develops its bouquet on the skin usually consists of twenty-five or more essential oils.

Inunctions & aroma massages

When diluted with high-quality fatty plant oils, essential oils are very well suited for inunctions and for different types of massages. Some essential oils have a relaxing effect on the muscles, e.g., marjoram, tangerine, or lavender. Rosemary, on the other hand, activates the circulation and improves the blood flow. If you know the effect of the active ingredients of essential oils you can increase the effect of massages.

Aroma bath

An aroma bath at the end of a demanding day can do wonders. The temperature of the water should not be over 100 degrees Fahrenheit. Disperse the essential oils emulsified with salt, honey, cream, or milk in the tub. A bath for an adult requires about ten drops of essential oils. For children, 5 drops are sufficient.

For a relaxing bath in the evening you should use soothing oils like lavender, tangerine, orange, neroli, vanilla, or benzoin. After the bath, you can wrap yourself in a blanket and rest or go directly to bed and fall into a good sleep with the calming bouquet of the oils in your nose.

Guidelines for safe application

• Essential oils are highly concentrated and with only a few exceptions (e.g., lavender and tea tree oil) should not be applied undiluted to the skin. The following guideline values as to dosage are recommended:
  • children (1–3 years):
    1 drop essential oil in 10 ml fatty basic oil
  • children (3–7 years):
    2 drops essential oil in 10 ml fatty basic oil
  • children (7–12 years):
    3 drops essential oil in 10 ml fatty basic oil
  • children (from 12 years):
    4 drops essential oil in 10 ml fatty basic oil
  • adults: 6 drops essential oil in 10 ml fatty basic oil (corresponds to a concentration of 3%)

• The above dosages do not apply to essential oils which are extracted with CO_2. According to the producers, these oils sometimes contain other active ingredients or other proportions among these ingredients. For adults, a 1% concentration for skin applications is recommended.

• Keep essential oils out of reach of children.

• Essential oils with a high content of eucalyptus (e.g., peppermint, eucalyptus globulus) should not be used with children under 6 years of age.

• Never use thyme, eucalyptus globulus, peppermint, or camphor with small children. These essential oils might cause a reaction with respiratory failure!

- Babies under 6 months should not be treated with essential oils except under special circumstances. Exceptions: rose oil diluted with almond or sesame oil, a 1% dilution of sandalwood in calendula oil in case of infantile eczema, lavender and neroli oil for restless babies. As to dosage, "less is more" applies, so use no more than 0.5% to 1% blends.
- Because babies cannot cough up phlegm on their own during the first few months they should never be given expectorant essential oils (e.g., eucalyptus, thyme, myrtle, etc.)—there is an acute danger of asphyxiation!
- Do not allow essential oils to get into the eyes or ears, do not touch any contact lenses, and don´t rub your eyes while there are oils on your fingers.
- In case of essential oil getting into the eyes, immediately rinse profusely with lots of water; running water is best. If you have any further complaints see a doctor.
- In case of pregnancy do not utilize the following oils without consulting with your physician first: basil, bay, savory, gromwell, vervain, tarragon, ginger, clove, camphor, marjoram, nutmeg, clary sage, myrrh, thyme, juniper, hyssop, cinnamon.
- In case of seizures and high blood pressure, always consult with a physician first. Do not use oils such as rosemary, thyme, salvia, hyssop, savory, and laurel.

- If you are prone to allergic reactions, first perform an allergy test on the inside of your forearm. Put a small amount of the essential oil onto the inside of your forearm. If there is any reaction after 24 hours do not use the oil.
- Essential oils should not be put directly into the bathwater, always mix it first with some natural bath gel, honey, milk, salt, or pure vegetable oil to emulsify.
- Always keep the oil flasks tightly closed and protected from light in a cool place.
- Essential oils like lemon, bergamot, orange, or other citrus oils may cause skin reactions or pigmentation (photosensitivity) when the skin is exposed to sunlight after applying oils.
- The sole of the foot is among the safest and most effective areas to apply oils.

This is only a brief introduction into the many possibilities, effects, and applications of essential oils. If you are curious to find out more, you can see a licensed aroma therapy professional to help you with personalized counseling regarding the selection and application of essential oils. This allows you to make sure that the intended effects are indeed happening.

Note:
Use only 100% pure essential oils of high quality. Before applying them, read the labels concerning possible contraindications and precautions (particularly in case of pregnancy, asthma, with children and babies, seniors, epileptics, high blood pressure, etc.). Stick to the indicated dosages. Less is more!

The use of essential oils can contribute to physical wellbeing. However, they do not replace a physician´s treatment in case of problems or diseases.

Cooking
with essential oils

The senses of smell and taste are very much interconnected. In fact, some languages have only one word for both smelling and tasting. The sense of taste and the sense of smell contribute to the quality of life; they are the chemical senses.

The first question asked when sitting together at a table is "How does it taste?" Actually, the question should be "How does it smell?" We have five distinct tastes: sweet, sour, salty, bitter, and umami. This last taste was discovered only in 1907 by the Japanese researcher Ikeda. Our sense of smell plays a fundamental role in our society. Smell and taste experiences are stored in our limbic system, which is also responsible for our memories and emotions. The aroma of cinnamon, clove, and vanilla reminds most of us of the holiday season and the baking of cookies. The sense of smell, captured by our nose, causes the production of digestive juices, which assist in digesting food.

Spices and herbs not only provide the right aroma and taste. There has always been a close connection between healing and cooking. Old manuscripts tell about the healing powers of herbs and aromatic spices. Prior generations were used to having an herb garden, not only for use in their kitchen but also for medicinal uses. But what to do if you can´t have

an herb garden or cannot purchase fresh herbs? You could give essential oils a try—you won't be disappointed!

However you use herbs and spices for healing, they should always remain part of your kitchen ingredients. Essential oils are simply a clever addition to the aroma kitchen and can complement a taste or replace several herbs and plants that might not be easily available during winter.

The magic touch—essential oils in the kitchen

The wonderful aroma of the essential oils is not only great for aroma therapy, it can also be used in the kitchen to refine the taste of dishes. In ancient Egypt, so-called aroma bowls were passed around, filled with pleasant herbs mixed with essential oils. They were intended to lift the mood and to increase the production of digestive juices. Aromatic food can open the heart and the mind. Combined with the aromas

we sense, good food allows us to enjoy life fully. At the same time the aromas and essences of spice oils and herbs assist our digestive process and fortify our immune system.

Quality, not quantity!

We like to use oils in the kitchen which have been extracted with the CO_2 method, as their aroma and taste are closest to those of the plant. We prefer to use oils from organic cultivation.

Essential oils have very special properties, which play an important role in their use in aroma therapy practice as well as in the aroma kitchen. They are volatile substances and vanish rather quickly. So always keep the bottles with the essential oils tightly closed. Due to the production process they are always highly concentrated substances that can only be applied directly to the skin in exceptional cases, such as essential lavender oil, as they may cause skin irritation. These oils are, therefore, used sparingly to enhance foods in the aroma kitchen. Essential oils do not contain fat and are not water soluble, so they need to be emulsified with a basic substance (e.g., honey, salt, vegetable oils, etc.) before they can be applied to water-based ingredients (in aroma kitchen or an aroma bath).

Basics of usage

As mentioned before, essential oils are not meant to replace spices, fresh herbs, or fruits. They are intended as an expansion and an addition to the preparation of dishes. Their effect is mostly to refine dishes. Essential oils, just like their plants of origin, can also increase appetite or have a beneficial impact on the digestion. Grapefruit is generally considered to be appetite-increasing, according to the reports from the aroma community; it is even applied in case of eating disorders.

Other herb oils include cilantro, cardamom and others. These herb and spice oils can also have a positive effect on the digestion. On the other hand, getting a whiff of vanilla can calm the craving for sweets, while mint is even regarded to be an appetite suppressant. Because of the fact that these oils are highly concentrated and volatile a few guidelines apply to achieve the desired results when spicing dishes:

• Less is more! Beware of overdosing—one drop too many can ruin the dish.

• Never apply essential oils directly to the food! They are not water-soluble, which is why we need emulsifiers or basic compounds to combine the essential oils with the water-based foods. Among these are fat oils such as sunflower seed oil, sesame or olive oil, cream, egg yolk, butter, sour cream, yogurt, mustard, vinegar, honey, sugar, salt, mayonnaise, and alcohol (e.g., brandy). Mix the required number of drops with the emulsifier (the process is called emulsification) and then apply this mix to the dish.

• In the case of very intense aromas, it is often sufficient to add only one drop of essential oil to a spoon and allow it to run off. The oil that adheres to the spoon can be used to flavor the dishes (called the "spoon method"). When the recipes in this book call for $1/2$ drop of an essential oil, this is one method to use.

• Another method for low dosage is the "toothpick method." Use a toothpick moistened with the oil to stir the food.

• Essential oils are volatile. So they should be added to the dish only shortly before serving. This is more important in the case of hot meals.

• When baking with essential oils you can apply a higher dosage due to the volatility; this way the taste is retained until the end of the baking process.

• It makes sense to create a selection of spice oils, flavored syrups, or salts yourself. It makes cooking with essential oils much easier. You can find recipes on pages 30–36.

Popular essential oils / Basic rules for the aroma kitchen

- Only use 100 % natural and pure essential oils.
- Essential oils derived from true organic cultivation are best
- We recommend the use of CO_2-extracted oils as their aroma is the closest to the natural scent.
- Because essential oils are highly concentrated substances, the following chart lists a few precautions.

- These precautions are in the context of a longer and regular use (e.g., daily over the course of a few weeks). When sufficiently diluted, spice oils in the aroma kitchen do not cause any unwanted side effects. However, as each individual is different, an allergic reaction or incompatibility cannot be ruled out entirely.

Essential oil	Aroma kitchen application	*Precautions
European basil (Ocimum basilicum ct. linalool)	spice oils, spice honey, spice salts for sauces	• not during pregnancy • not for babies and toddlers
Bay oil (Pimenta racemosa)	spice oils, spice honey, and to refine Asian dishes with soy sauce	• not during pregnancy • not for babies and toddlers • no continuous application • no long-duration application in high doses when blood coagulation problems are present or medication for these is being taken • insufficient dilution the oil can have a an irritating effect on skin and mucous membranes
Bergamot (Citrus bergamia)	spice oils, spice honey, spice salts for sauces; great for fish and vegetables, tea (Earl Grey)	• when applied to the skin, avoid sunlight for at least 8 hours to eliminate the risk of sun spots or sunburn • during applications on the skin, irritations may occur due to overdosage, oxidization, and in combination with warm water (e.g., aroma bath)
Winter savory (Satureja montana)	spice oils, spice salts, spice butter; good for vegetables (green beans)	• use very low dose • not during pregnancy • oil can be irritating to skin or mucuous membranes if not sufficiently diluted

Essential oil	Aroma kitchen application	*Precautions
Blood orange *(Citrus sinensis)*	spice oils, spice honey, syrup, to refine desserts	• when applying to the skin avoid sunlight for at least 8 hours (spots can easily form as well as sunburn) • during applications on the skin, irritations may occur due to overdosage, oxidization, and in combination with warm water (e.g., aroma bath)
Dill oil *(Anethum graveolens)*	spice oils, spice salts, spice butter; good for vegetables and fish	• not during pregnancy • not for babies and toddlers
Tarragon *(Artemisia dracunculus)*	sauces, vegetable dishes, spice butter	• not for babies and toddlers • no long-term application • use as a 0.5% spice oil in the aroma kitchen
Geranium *(Pelargonium graveolens)*	syrup, spice honey, to refine desserts or appetizers (e.g., champagne with syrup)	• well tolerated when applied normally
Grapefruit *(Citrus paradisi)*	spice oils, spice honey, syrup, to refine desserts, to conserve jams or syrup	• when applying to the skin avoid sunlight for at least 8 hours (spots can easily form as well as sunburn) • during applications on the skin, irritations may occur due to overdosage, oxidization, and in combination with warm water (e.g., aroma bath)
Ginger CO_2-extracted *(Zingiber officinal)*	particularly to refine Asian dishes or to refine fish and squash dishes	• note: extremely spicy—use very low dosage, the toothpick method is best, or the muceous membranes may be irritated • with insufficient dilution the oil can be irritating for skin and muceous membranes • be careful in cases of blood coagulation problems or when taking medication for these • not during pregnancy

Essential oil	Aroma kitchen application	*Precautions
Distilled ginger (*Zingiber officinalis*)	mainly for refining Asian dishes or fish and squash dishes	• be careful in cases of blood coagulation problems or when taking medication for these • not during pregnancy
Coffee CO₂-extracted (*Coffee arabica*)	to refine desserts, coffee, and for baking	• no problems when used normally
Cocoa extract (*Theobroma cacao*)	to refine desserts, coffee, and for baking	• no problem when used normally
Cardamom (*Elletaria cardomomum*)	spice oils, especially to refine Arabic or Indian dishes, to refine sauces for fish and meat	• no problems when used normally
Cilantroseed oil (*Coriandrum sativum*)	spice oils, particularly to refine Arabic or Indian dishes, to refine sauces for fish and meat and for soups	• no problems when used normally
Garlic oil (*Allium sativum*)	spice oils, to refine salad dressings, particularly good for persons who avoid fresh garlic, no typical body odor as when consuming fresh garlic	• only used in the aroma kitchen • no problems when used normally
Cumin oil (*Cuminum cyminum*)	spice oils, spice salts; great for all Oriental dishes	• not during pregnancy • when applying to the skin avoid sunlight for at least 8 hours (spots can easily form as well as sunburn) • during applications on the skin, irritations may occur due to overdosage

Essential oil	Aroma kitchen application	*Precautions
Lavendel (*Lavandula officinalis/ angustifolia*)	to refine desserts, spreads, for making syrup and to flavor ice cream	• no problems when used normally
Lemongrass (*Cymbopogon flexuosus*)	spice oils, spice salts; great for all Asian dishes, particularly Thai with coconut milk, great as a spice salt for fish dishes	• persons with increased eye pressure (glaucoma) should not use this essential oil too often • during applications on the skin, irritations may occur due to overdosage, oxidization, and in combination with warm water (e.g., aroma bath)
Pressed lime (*Citrus aurantifolia*)	spice oils, spice salts, for syrup (e.g., to refine elderberry syrup), to flavor ice cream and other desserts as well as fish sauces and chicken	• when applying to the skin avoid sunlight for at least 8 hours (spots can easily form as well as sunburn) • during applications on the skin, irritations may occur due to overdosage, oxidization, and in combination with warm water (e.g., aroma bath)
Laurel leaves (*Laurus nobilis*)	spice oils, particularly for olives etc., and to refine sauces for venison and fish	• only under professional supervision during pregnancy • depending on its composition and origin, skin applications may cause irritation
Marjoram, CO₂-extracted (*Origanum majorana*)	spice oils, to refine Italian dishes	• do not overdose this essential oil in the kitchen during pregnancy
Red tangerine (*Citrus reticulata*)	spice oils, spice syrup, to refine desserts, syrups, appetizers and for fish and vegetables in combination with spice oils	• when applying to the skin avoid sunlight for at least 8 hours (spots can easily form as well as sunburn) • during applications on the skin, irritations may occur due to overdosage, oxidization, and in combination with warm water (e.g., aroma bath)

Essential oil	Aroma kitchen application	*Precautions
Clary sage *(Salvia sclarea)*	spice salts, to refine vegetables, venison or fish dishes	• not during pregnancy • not in cases of estrogen-dependent precancers • boosts the effect of alcohol • not in cases of endometriosis • not during heavy menstruation
Nutmeg oil *(Myristica fragrans)*	spice oils, to refine dishes, particularly vegetable dishes and mashed potatoes	• use the oil only sparingly and occasionally; an overdose can cause hallucinogenic effects • not during pregnancy
Clove buds *(Syzigium aromaticum)*	to refine desserts, coffee and for baking, for venison, red cabbage, etc.	• not during pregnancy • no long-term application in high doses in cases of blood coagulation problems and/or blood-thinning medication • if not sufficiently diluted the oil may cause irritation of the skin and mucous membranes • not for babies and children • no long-term application
Neroli *(Citrus aurantium flos.)*	for exquisite sweet dishes and syrups	• no problems when used normally
Sweet orange *(Citrus sinensis)*	spice oils, spice salts and spice syrups to refine sweet dishes; great for fish when combined with spice oils	• when applying to the skin avoid solarium or sunlight for at least 8 hours (spots can easily form as well as sunburn) • during applications on the skin, irritations may occur due to overdosage, oxidization, and in combination with warm water (e.g., aroma bath)
Black pepper *(Piper nigrum)*	any dish where you use the spice itself, but also for strawberry jam or in combination with orange oil for black chocolate	• note: during applications on the skin, irritations may occur due to overdosage, oxidization, and in combination with warm water (e.g., aroma bath)

Essential oil	Aroma kitchen application	*Precautions
Peppermint *(Mentha piperita)*	spice syrup, to refine juices, ice cubes, desserts, etc.	• only under professional medical care during pregnancy • not for children under 6 years—replace with spearmint *(Mentha spicata)* • not in cases of epilepsy • note: during applications on the skin, irritations may occur due to overdosage, oxidization, and in combination with warm water (e.g., aroma bath) • not for sufferers of asthma • not in combination with homeopathic treatments
Bulgarian rose *(Rosa damascena)*	spice salt, spice honey, spice syrup, to refine juices, ice cubes, desserts, etc.	• no problems when used normally
Rosemary *(Rosmarinus officinalis)*	spice oils, spice salts, to refine meat and fish dishes	• only with professional medical supervision in cases of pregnancy • no high dosage in cases of high blood pressure • not for children under 6 years • not in cases of epilepsy
Sage *(Salvia officinalis)*	spice oils, spice salts, to refine meats and fish	• not during pregnancy • not in cases of epilepsy
Thyme ct. linalool *(Thymus vulgaris ct. linalool)*	spice oils, spice salts, to refine meats and fish	• only with professional medical supervision in cases of pregnancy
Tonka bean *(Dipteryx odorata)*	spice syrup, to refine desserts and alcoholic beverages	• no problems when used normally
Vanilla extract *(Vanilla planifolia)*	to refine desserts, coffee and for baking, venison, red cabbage, etc.	• no problems when used normally

Essential oil	Aroma kitchen application	*Precautions
Juniper (*Juniperus communis*)	spice oils, spice salts, to refine meats (e.g., venison) and vegetables (e.g., red cabbage)	• only with professional medical supervision in cases of pregnancy
Ylang-ylang (*Cananga odorata*)	to refine desserts	• no long-term application in cases of low blood pressure • high dosage can lead to headaches • note: during applications on the skin, irritations may occur due to overdosage, oxidization, and in combination with warm water (e.g., aroma bath)
Cinnamon bark (*Cinnamomum verum*)	to refine desserts, coffee and for baking, for venison, red cabbage, etc.	• not during pregnancy • may cause mucous membrane irritation if not sufficiently diluted • for children, only use in aroma lamps • no long-term application in high dosages in case of blood coagulation problems and/or taking blood-thinning medication • no long-term application
Lemon (*Citrus limonum*)	spice salt, spice honey, spice syrup, to flavor juices, ice cubes, desserts, etc.; great for fish dishes and vegetables	• when applying to the skin avoid sunlight for at least 8 hours (spots can easily form as well as sunburn) • note: during applications on the skin, irritations may occur due to overdosage, oxidization, and in combination with warm water (e.g., aroma bath)

* the indicated precautions regarding essential oils are based on the available medical literature.

Hydrolates in the aroma kitchen

Hydrolates are products derived from the process of making essential oils. They contain the water-soluble parts of the plant and only a small amount of essential oil. Hydrolates can be used in the aroma kitchen to gently season and flavor dishes and salads. When shopping, make sure the hydrolates are not diluted with alcohol and that they are bottled in 100 ml spray bottles. Hydrolates should be stored in the refrigerator and can be used for about eight weeks after their first use.

Hydrolate	Application in the aroma kitchen
Rose hydrolate	to refine beverages, sauces, desserts, salad dressings; particularly suited for leaf lettuce and white meat
Lavender hydrolate	to refine beverages, sauces, desserts, salad dressings; great for flavoring homemade ice cream or frozen yogurt
Rosemary hydrolate	to refine sauces and salad dressings
Orange flower hydrolate	to refine beverages, sauces, desserts, salad dressings; great for leaf lettuce, white meat, and fish as well as venison sauces

Oriental butter

½ lb butter
½ tsp sea salt
3 drp cilantroseed oil
1 drp cardamom oil
1 drp cinnamon oil, CO_2-extracted
        (explanation on page 11)
½ tsp cumin (ground)

Take the butter from the refrigerator 1 hour
before preparation and place in a mixing bowl
(it becomes softer and is easier to work with).
Put the sea salt onto a teaspoon, put the
essential oil on the salt, and blend with the
cumin powder and the butter.

Separate the butter you will use during
the next few days (good for 3 to 4 days) and
freeze the rest of the oriental butter, divided
into convenient portions. Oriental butter is
great for seasoning fried vegetables, oven
potatoes, or grilled chicken.

Rose butter

½ lb soft butter
2 tbsp rose water (or 1 drp rose oil)
8 aromatic rose leaves, finely chopped
• salt

Beat the butter with a blender until foamy and add
rose water or rose oil. Remove the white section
from the rose leaves, cut into thin strips and mix
with the butter; add salt.

Seasoned salts

Blood orange-lemongrass salt

6 drp lemongrass oil
8 drp blood orange oil
¼ C sea salt

Place the essential oils into a dark screw top jar
with about ¼-cup capacity and turn the container
so that the oil spreads along the inside. Add ¼
cup of sea salt, shake well, and leave for a few
days. Continue to shake every few days. After
2 weeks the salt has absorbed the essential oils
and can be used in the aroma kitchen.

Lavender salt

  ½ C sea salt
2 tbsp dried lavender flowers
15 drp lavender oil

Great for the Mediterranean kitchen.

Pepper-orange salt

  ½ C sea salt
- dried orange zests of a small orange
- some peppercorns

10 drp orange oil
 9 drp black pepper oil

Prepare like rose salt. Great as a finishing salt for steaks and poultry.

Rose salt

  ½ C coarse sea salt
2 tbsp dried rose leaves
 5 drp rose oil

Place essential oil into a screw-top jar and proceed as with the blood orange-lemongrass salt. Fill with salt and leave for a few days. Cut the salt with the rose leaves and put into an airtight jar. Great as finishing salt for poultry, fish, and salads.

BLOOD ORANGE–LEMONGRASS TIP:
Instead of blood orange oil you can use orange oil; this tends to make the taste of the spice salt more round and warm. You can also use a fruit peel mix instead of blood orange oil. This adds freshness and a fruit aroma to the mix.

Ginger salt

  ½ C sea salt
  1 nut-sized piece of dry ginger
15 drp ginger oil

Great for Asian dishes.

Vanilla sugar

½ C brown cane sugar or white sugar
50 drp vanilla extract in alcohol (10:90)

Put the sugar into a dark screw top jar with 1-cup capacity and sprinkle the vanilla extract over it. Stir with a wooden stick or spoon.
    After 2 weeks the sugar will have absorbed the essential oil and is now ready to be used for baking in the aroma kitchen.

Rose sugar

½ C sugar
10 drp rose oil
2 tbsp dried rose leaves

Rinse the walls of the screw-top jar with the essential oil. Add sugar and shake well. Leave to mature, and mix with the dried rose leaves.

TIP:
As brown sugar has its own distinctive taste, you might want to use white sugar for these recipes.

Orange sugar

½ C brown sugar or white sugar
• dried zests of an orange
20 drp orange oil

Prepare just like rose sugar.

Helpful tricks for aroma chefs

Flavored containers and cooking utensils

Dishes can be nicely flavored by rubbing some essential oil onto the cutting boards and into the bowls and containers where foods are prepared. Rub 3–5 drops of various citrus oils or 1–2 drops of any other essential oil on the cutting board that is used for cutting vegetables or meat. For bowls and other containers where foods are prepared, 1-3 drops of essential oil are applied.

Painting and brushing

As soon as you remove some fresh pastries, a cake or soufflé, a quiche or a pizza, from the oven, you can paint them with aromatic seasoned oils while they are still warm. This allows for dishes to be deliciously refined and provides an enchanting aroma.

A very simple yet efficient method is to provide an aroma brush, such as rosemary or thyme twigs. Dip them into the seasoned oil and place them on the table. Your guests can help themselves to flavor their own dishes.

Seeds with aromatic seasoned salt

Actually all fat-containing nuts and seeds are good carriers for essential oils. Here is a variation to sprinkle over salads or as a delicious topping for buttered bread.

Roast separately equal parts (¼ lb. each) of sesame, sunflower, and pumpkin seeds. Chop the pumpkin seeds coarsely so their size matches that of the other ingredients.

Place the seeds into a jar and add 1 tsp of seasoned salt of your choice or simply sea salt. Leave for two weeks.

Flavored meringues for pastries

You can add a special something to cakes with meringues by refining them with a teaspoon of flavored honey, a tablespoon of fruit or vanilla sugar, or 1–3 drops of citrus oils of your choice. Spread the flavored beaten egg white evenly on the cake and finish baking.

Tips for using this cookbook

Layout of the cookbook

Initially, this cookbook´s recipe section follows the classic structure:

- Appetizers
- Soups
- Main dishes
- Side dishes
- Desserts

However, this just was not good enough for us. For every main dish you will find suggestions as to which side dishes from our book are great to go along with it. We have also added variations for many dishes. Some of the recipes can be easily converted into a vegetarian or vegan version. Things get really exciting when there is an upcoming occasion to offer a menu that captivates the guests. This is why you will find an additional chapter dedicated to special occasions. We also provide helpful tips about how to sail smoothly through an evening with several guests. The recipes in our cookbook are intended for four people.

Seasonal & regional ingredients

"You are what you eat." A true, wise saying. We put particular emphasis on high quality. Regional organic products are preferred, and we avoid instant and processed food products as much as possible. We really prefer to purchase our products from local farmers and growers whom we know and trust. In the case of foreign products, we make sure they are from sustainable agriculture and we prefer organic and fair trade products. With fruits and vegetables we try to use seasonal products that are available in our area at any given time.

There are many who underestimate the variety of winter vegetables available as either fresh or high-quality stored produce. Vitamin C, dietary fiber, and sufficient folic acid are particularly important during the winter season to strengthen our immune systems. Instead of getting your bell pepper from Spain, with the associated CO_2 emissions, you should buy winter and storable vegetables locally. Because there is quite a considerable selection of all kinds of vegetables during late fall and winter: cabbage, pumpkin, carrots, leeks, red beets, corn salad, endives, and many more. Look for your local growers and farmers´ market, which provide fresh produce year-round from your area. This not only assures freshness but the short transport distances are good for the environment, too. With fruit it is not quite as simple to get regional, fresh fruit all year round.

In the United States there is a good supply of a variety of fruits from April to December. They range from rhubarb in spring to the many kinds of berries in summer, apples, pears and plums in autumn, to quince, which can be available until early December. A particular favorite, available year-round, is the apple. The characteristic fruity, sweet and aromatic scent of apples is attractive to almost everyone. You can eat the many sweet and tart varieties raw, as a delicious vitamin provider, or bake, fry and cook them.

High-quality vegetable oils

We put a high value on using high-quality, and if possible native, cold-pressed vegetable oils. They retain all of the vitamins and fats that are important for our metabolisms. They also have a very distinct taste which refines the dishes.

"Native" is related to the production process of vegetable oils and includes purity of variety, first pressing, no extraction, no refining, and no other post-processing except for filtering.

Mechanical or hydraulic pressing is the most gentle method for native vegetable oils. Seeds, nuts, or fruits are chopped mechanically, slightly warmed up in a pan, and pressed with hydraulic compression cylinders. Then the oil is either filtered or it is allowed to rest for a certain period while the suspended particles in the oil settle at the bottom and the remaining oil can be bottled without impurities. Generally, native oils only allow for pressing, washing, centrifuging, and filtering their production.

Only these steps allow the oils to retain their full quality, their vitamins, lecithin, aromatic compounds, fatty acids, and much more.

Cold-pressed oils

The term "cold-pressed," by the way, is not a registered trademark! However, for olive oil there is a EU guideline which defines the production process and labeling. These production processes during cold-pressing are non-destructive but require much time, and the resulting amount of oil is a lot lower than when hot-pressing or extracting. With those methods, the plants are heated and much more oil is extracted while adding solvents. However, this process changes the molecular fat chains and may leave behind residual solvents.

Refined oils

These are chemically cleaned fatty oils. The end result is a clear, neutral, and storable oil. However, this process destroys a large part of the important vitamins and fatty components. Sunflower or corn oils from the supermarket which are marketed for frying or deep-frying consist of refined oils. If you use native vegetable oils, be aware of the fact that not all vegetable oils can be heated!

Particularly suited for frying or deep-frying (good heat stability):
- native organic coconut oil

For stewing and gentle frying:
- native organic olive oil
- native organic sesame oil
- native organic peanut oil
- native organic grapeseed oil

The following native vegetable oils should not be heated. You can use then for salads and sauces or season warm dishes with them:
- native organic thistle oil
- native organic hemp oil
- native organic hazelnut oil
- native organic pumpkin seed oil
- native organic linseed oil
- native organic macadamia nut oil
- native organic almond oil
- native organic poppyseed oil
- native organic canola oil
- native organic sunflower oil
- native organic walnut oil

Better to avoid
We never use margarine or processed fats and oils. They are cheaper, heat resistant, and can be stored long-term. But at what cost? The industrial production of vegetable oils is usually done through chemical extraction, as the yield is about 99% higher when compared to native cold pressing. Elaborate chemical and thermal processes (refining) clean the raw material (fats and oils) while destroying a large part of the precious substances and vitamins. This means that the final product is a clear, storable oil which is neutral as to smell and taste.

Margarine is based on processed, refined vegetable oils, water, and various emulsifiers. As vegetable oils are liquid at room temperature, the margarine receives an additional hardening process. The addition of emulsifiers makes the margarine spreadable.

The last step consists of adding color and preservative substances as well as vitamins. All of these steps change the original fat composition in a significant way. For example, the heating processes produce trans fats, which cannot be metabolized by the body.

Watch for quality
Our motto, therefore, is why use denaturized foods if nature already provides everything we need? Healthy, clean, fully matured seeds, the experience and the magic touch of the pressing masters and the traditional press are the elements from which the perfect drop is produced.

Sugar

Sugar is also a hotly debated issue. There are many of us who love sweet dishes and we don´t really like to skip the "sweet sin" after a meal. There are a variety of delicious desserts presented in our aroma cookbook.

In order for diabetics and calorie-conscious people to be able to savor our delicacies we can offer a little-known alternative to sugar—"birch sugar," also called xylitol. Xylitol was discovered in 1891 by the German chemist Emil Fischer. "Birch sugar" is a sugar substitute which belongs to the group of sugar alcohols. It is produced using chemical processes (catalytic hydrogenation) from wood sugar (xylose). The common term "birch sugar" is used because the initial production was from Finnish birch. Actually, natural "birch sugar" is part of many fruits, berries, trees, vegetables, and grains. Industrial birch sugar is produced today using corncobs

(without grains). In this case, it is important that the corn is from non-GMO cultivation.

The production of birch sugar is technically demanding and elaborate, partiuclarly so if a pure product is desired, so this sugar is more expensive than common sugar.

The advantages over conventional sugar are obvious:
• "Birch sugar" has the same sweetening power as sugar and requires no change as to use and dosage.
• The nutritional value of 2.4 calories per gram is about 40% less than conventional sugar.
• Birch sugar acts independently of insulin in the human metabolism and hence it is useful for diabetics.
• Birch sugar is contained as a natural substance in plants. It is produced as a byproduct of the glucose metabolism.
• Birch sugar is a sugar replacement, not an artificial sweetener, such as aspartame and saccharin.
• Unlike sugar, birch sugar has an alkaline effect on the body. It decreases the growth of bacteria. The reseach into tooth decay has shown that the regular use of birch sugar (contained in chewing gum or lozenges) reduced the formation of cavities.
• The sugar replacement is suitable for children.

The only limitations of birch sugar is that some animal species, such as dogs, do not tolerate birch sugar and it is not suitable for baking goods made from yeast dough.

The caramelization temperature of birch sugar is about 390° Fahrenheit. So you can replace sugar with birch sugar in almost all of our recipes for sweet dishes.

Time indications and level of difficulty

The time indications for our recipes are divided into preparation time (the time needed to prepare the dish), the cooking time (during which you can do other things) and waiting time (to marinate, cool down, harden...).

If you combine a main dish with a side dish you need not necessarily add up the indicated preparation times. In many cases you can combine individual steps or do other tasks and reduce the total time.

Example

Main dish: Aristo pork filet
   (45 min. without marinating time)
Side dish: Oriental carrot rice (15 min.)
Total time: 45 min.

Peel and cut the carrots before starting to braise the meat. With the meat in the oven, cook the rice and saute the carrots in the frying pan. The rice and meat are ready at about the same time. Take the meat out of the oven and leave to rest. Mix rice and carrots, season and keep warm. Prepare the sauce and serve. Total time: 45 minutes.

The difficulty of the dishes is indicated by easy, medium, and elaborate. We want to make your culinary planning and expedition into the realm of the aroma kitchen as simple as possible. Have a lot of fun while making these recipes come to life!

Recipes

Cold Appetizers

All recipes are for 4 portions

Avocado Salad with Shrimp and Lime Oil Dressing

PREPARATION TIME: 40 min.   •   **WAITING TIME:** 2–3 hours   •   **DIFFICULTY:** Easy

INGREDIENTS

1	ripe avocado
1	red bell pepper
1	green bell pepper
•	a few black olives (without pits)
1	small red onion
4 oz	Gouda cheese
200 g	shrimp, cooked

MARINADE

4 tbsp	balsamic vinegar
1 pinch	sea salt
1 pinch	black pepper
8 tbsp	olive oil
3–4 drp	lime oil

• Cut avocado in half, remove pit, remove pulp, and cut into small cubes, set aside the skin.
• Wash bell peppers, remove seeds, and cut into small pieces. Mince the olives. Peel onions and finely chop. Last, cut Gouda into small cubes.

• For the marinade, put balsamic vinegar, salt, and pepper into a salad bowl and blend thoroughly. Emulsify the lime oil with the olive oil and add to the balsamic vinegar; blend again.
• Combine the shrimp wih the prepared ingredients; add to the bowl with the marinade and stir. Leave in the refrigerator for 2–3 hours.
• Remove salad from the refrigerator 30 minutes before serving, and place into the avocado skins or serve in small bowls with toasted bread triangles.

TIP:
For the vegan variation, simply skip the shrimp and replace the Gouda with high-quality tofu.

TIP:
You can replace the shrimp with crawfish.

Tomato and Avocado Carpaccio

5–6 tomatoes
2 avocados
½ lb soft cheese (local goat or sheep cheese)
1 pinch lemon salt (see page 36)

MARINADE

2 tbsp balsamic vinegar
½ drp garlic oil (spoon method; see page 21)
2 tbsp olive oil
1 tbsp lemon seasoning oil (see page 32)

PREPARATION TIME: 20 min. • **DIFFICULTY:** Easy

• Cut tomatoes into very thin slices (a knife for cutting bread or a ceramic knife works great). Peel avocados and cut into thin slices, and cut the cheese into thin wafers as well.
• Arrange decoratively on a plate and serve, adding some lemon salt.

• Flavor the balsamic vinegar with a touch of garlic oil for the marinade, and drip over the prepared ingredients. Leave at least for half an hour.
• Add olive oil and lemon seasoning oil over the carpaccio.

TIP:
Serve with fresh white bread.

Couscous Salad

INGREDIENTS

1 cup couscous
1 red bell pepper
1 shallot
• a few olives
3 drp orange oil
1 drp peppermint oil
3 tbsp sesame oil
1 small orange
• a few raisins
¼ C almonds
• pepper-orange salt (see page 35)
2 tbsp vinegar

PREPARATION TIME: 20 min. • **DIFFICULTY:** Easy

• Pour 2 cups boiling water over the couscous and leave to soak for about 20 minutes. Meanwhile, wash the bell pepper and finely chop. Also chop the shallot and the olives.
• Emulsify the essential oils with the sesame oil. Peel and fillet the orange; emulsify the prepared ingredients

with raisins and almonds then add the emulsified seasoning oil to the cooked couscous and mix well.
• Refine with pepper-orange salt and vinegar and serve in small bowls.

TIP:
If you add a few drops of chili spice oil it will provide a unique taste!

Leaf Salad with Orange Vinaigrette

INGREDIENTS

½ lb mixed seasonal
salad greens (corn
salad, arugula, red
endive, lettuce)

VINAIGRETTE

4 tbsp balsamic vinegar
1 pinch sea salt
8 tbsp cold-pressed
organic
sunflower
or thistle oil
3–4 drp orange oil

PREPARATION TIME: 15 min. • **DIFFICULTY:** Easy

• Wash ingredients, dry with a salad spinner and tear into adequately sized pieces.
• For the vinaigrette, mix the balsamic vinegar with the salt in a salad bowl. Emulsify the sunflower or thistle oil with the orange oil, add to the balsamic vinegar, and mix well in a blender.
• Place the leaf salad into a bowl, mix with the vinaigrette, and serve right away so the greens remain crisp.

TIP:
Leaf salads have only a little taste of their own, the tasty seasoning is provided by the marinade, vinaigrette, or dressing. To make sure that every leaf of the salad is mixed with the vinaigrette it is best to toss leaf salad by hand.

TIP:
Alternatively, instead of the sunflower or thistle oil, you can use the Sicilian seasoning oil (page 31) or the lemon seasoning oil (page 32) with the essential orange oil.

Mozzarella Skewers with Prosciutto

INGREDIENTS

½ lb baby mozzarella
12 slices of prosciutto
12 cherry tomatoes
and olives
• basil leaves
3 tbsp white balsamic
vinegar
• salt and pepper
1 pinch cane sugar
½ tbsp lemon seasoning oil
(see page 32)
2–3 tbsp olive oil

PREPARATION TIME: 20 min. • **MARINATING TIME:** 20 min. • **DIFFICULTY:** Easy

• Stick the baby-mozzarella, prosciutto, cherry tomatoes, olives, and basil leaves alternatingly onto wooden skewers.
• For the marinade, mix the vinegar, salt, pepper, and cane sugar. Emulsify the lemon oil with the olive oil and blend well with the marinade.
• Drip the marinade onto the skewers before serving.

TIP:
The skewers look really nice if you alternate yellow and red cherry tomatoes.

TIP:
Soak the skewers in water for 20 minutes before using them.

Arugula Salad with Lemon Vinaigrette

INGREDIENTS

½ lb arugula
¾ C Parmesan cheese
4 slices ham (optional)

VINAIGRETTE
8 tbsp olive oil
3–4 drp lemon oil
4 tbsp balsamic vinegar
• salt and black
pepper
1 apple

PREPARATION TIME: 20 min. • **DIFFICULTY:** Easy

• Wash the arugula and dry in a salad spinner.
• Emulsify the olive oil with the lemon oil and mix in a salad bowl with the balsamic vinegar, salt, and pepper, using a whisk to make a vinaigrette.
• Peel the apple and grate it directly into the vinaigrette.
• Add the arugula and mix with the vinaigrette, gradually adding freshly grated Parmesan cheese.

• Arrange on salad plates with grissini (bread sticks), toast triangles, and/or thinly sliced prosciutto.

TIP:
Instead of the essential lemon oil emulsified with the olive oil, you can use 8 tbsp of lemon seasoning oil (see page 32).

Asian Quark Spread

INGREDIENTS

1 C quark (or use cottage cheese)
1 tsp curry powder
1 pinch sea salt
2 drp lemongrass oil
1 tbsp native sesame oil
• lemon thyme or capers for garnishing

TIP:
If you like it hot, flavor the spread with a few drops of chili spice oil. Careful—very hot!

• Mix the quark or cottage cheese with the curry powder and the sea salt. Emulsify the lemongrass oil with the sesame oil and add to the quark while stirring. Leave in the refrigerator for 2–3 hours.
• Take the spread from the refrigerator at least 30 minutes before serving so that the aroma can develop, then serve on baguette or pumpernickel slices; garnish with fresh sprigs of lemon thyme or capers.

TIP:
Instead of 2 drops of lemongrass oil you can also refine with a pinch of blood orange-lemongrass salt (see page 34). Nevertheless, add the sesame oil as it makes the spread smooth and provides a nice aroma.

Spicy-Hot Lentil Spread

¾ C   red lentils
1   small piece of ginger
3   garlic cloves
1   small onion
1 tbsp   olive oil for braising
½ tsp   mustard seeds
•   salt and pepper
2 tbsp   olive oil to emulsify
1 drp   each of ginger oil,
            lemongrass oil,
            cinnamon oil,
            cilantro oil
1 tsp   turmeric
1   chili pepper
½ drp   cumin oil
4–5 tbsp   sour cream

PREPARATION TIME: 30 min.   •   **DIFFICULTY:** Easy

• Cook lentils for about 20 minutes. Meanwhile, peel the ginger and cut into small cubes; chop garlic.
• Chop the onion and braise in olive oil; add ginger and garlic as well as mustard seeds and braise together until the seeds pop.

• Mix in the boiled lentils and cook.
• Emulsify the spread with salt, pepper, and the essential oils emulsified in 2 tbsp of olive oil; season and mash. Add turmeric, finely chopped chili pepper without seeds, cumin oil, and sour cream.

Lavender Cream Cheese

1-2 drp   lavender oil
1-2 tbsp   olive oil
8 oz   cream cheese
1 pinch   sea salt
•   a few dried
        lavender flowers
        for garnishing

PREPARATION TIME: 15 min.   •   **WAITING TIME:** 2–3 hours   •   **DIFFICULTY:** Easy

• Emulsify the essential lavender oil with the olive oil and mix well with the cream cheese. Season with sea salt and refrigerate for 2–3 hours.
• Take out of the refrigerator at least 30 minutes before serving, so the aroma can develop.

• Serve the spread on small toasted bread triangles or pumpernickel slices; garnish with lavender flowers.

TIP:
This lavender cream cheese is great for an Italian appetizer dish with Parmesan cheese, grilled vegetables, and prosciutto. Serve with grissini or ciabatta.

Hummus

INGREDIENTS

1	can of chickpeas (8 oz)
½ C	vegetable broth
4 tbsp	olive oil
1-2 drp	garlic oil
2 drp	lemon oil
½ drp	cumin oil
½ drp	peppermint oil
•	salt, pepper
1 tbsp	chopped parsley
2 tbsp	roasted sesame seeds
⅔ C	sour cream

PREPARATION TIME: 20 min.
DIFFICULTY: Easy

• Set aside 3 tbsp of the chickpeas and mash the rest with the soup.
• Emulsify the olive oil with the essential oils; mix all of the ingredients together and season to taste with salt and pepper. Garnish with reserved chickpeas.

TIP:
If you like it hot, flavor the spread with a few drops of chili spice oil. Careful—very hot!

Sheep Cheese Provençal

INGREDIENTS

½ lb	sheep cheese
2 tbsp	Provençal seasoning oil
2	red apples
•	juice of ½ a lemon
•	crackers or tortilla chips

PREPARATION TIME: 20 min.
DIFFICULTY: Easy

• Cut cheese into small cubes, add seasoning oil, and mash to a paste with a fork.
• Wash apples, remove center with a corer, and cut crosswise into 4 thick slices; sprinkle them with lemon juice.
• Use a teaspoon to put a dollop of cheese onto each slice, and serve with crackers or tortilla chips.

Thai-Egg Spread

INGREDIENTS

4	hard-boiled eggs
⅔ C	crème fraîche
⅔ C	mayonnaise (light)
1 tbsp	tarragon mustard
2 tsp	curry powder
1 tbsp	sesame oil
2–3 drp	lemongrass oil
1 pinch	sea salt
•	lemon thyme or parsley leaves for garnishing

PREPARATION TIME: 15 min.
WAITING TIME: 2–3 hours
DIFFICULTY: Easy

• Peel the cooled eggs and chop finely. Mix crème fraîche, mayonnaise, tarragon mustard, and curry powder. Emulsify the sesame oil with the lemongrass oil and mix in. Add the chopped eggs.
• Season with a pinch of sea salt and leave in the refrigerator for 2–3 hours. Take out of the refrigerator at least 30 minutes before serving, so the aroma can develop.

TIP:
If you use sour cream instead of crème fraîche the result is a thick sauce which is great as a dip for grilled dishes, fondue, or boiled potatoes.

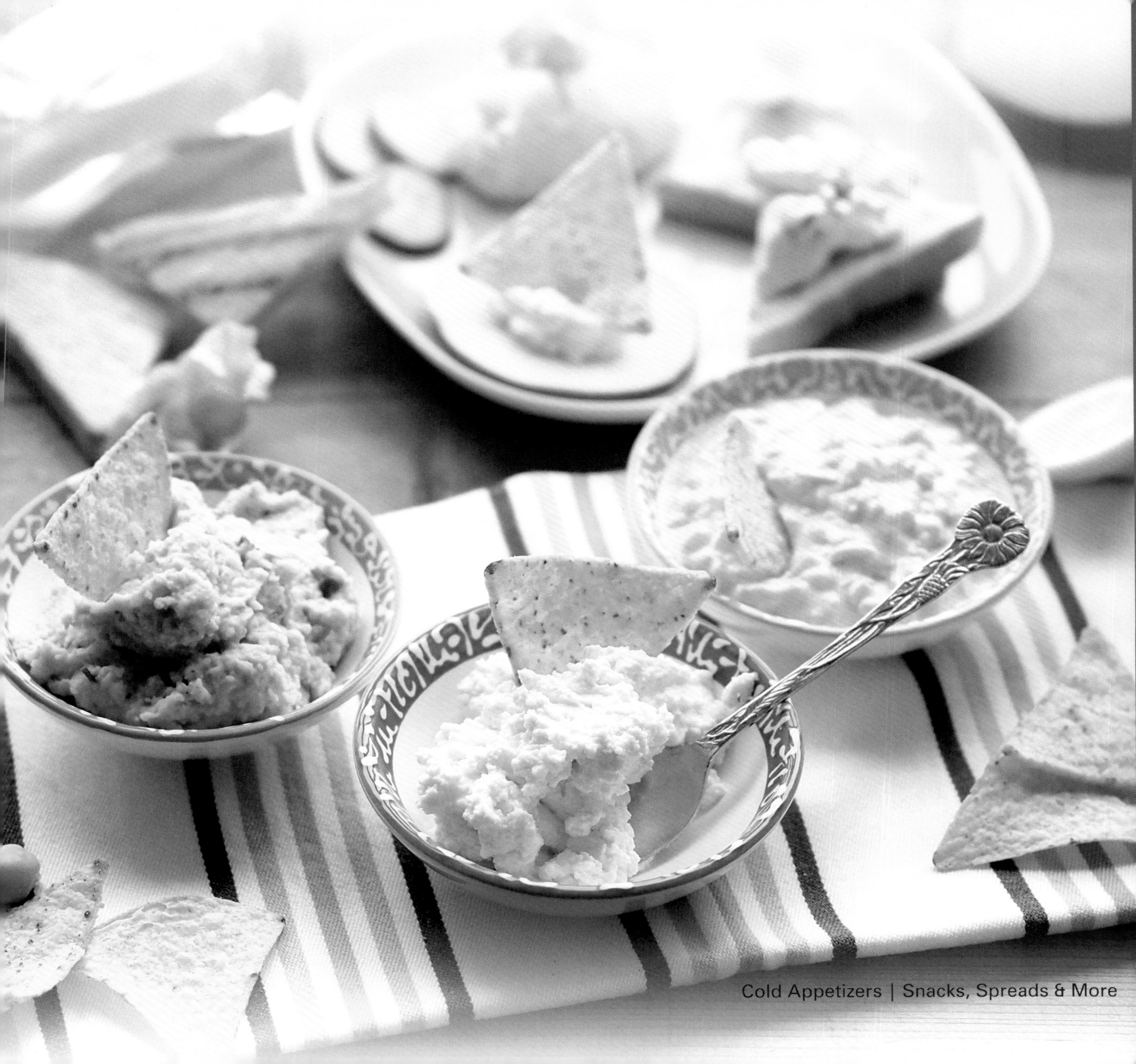

Vegetable Skewers with Rose Marinade

INGREDIENTS

- 12 cherry tomatoes
- 1 yellow bell pepper
- 1 small salad cucumber
  (or 1 green bell pepper)
- radishes (seasonal)
  optional
- 12 mozzarella balls
- fresh basil leaves

MARINADE

- 6 tbsp balsamic vinegar
- 12 tbsp olive oil
- 1 pinch sea salt
- some rose hydrolate
  (available in spray
  bottles)

- 4 wooden skewers (8")

PREPARATION TIME: 30 min. • **MARINATING TIME:** 20 Min. • **DIFFICULTY:** Easy

- Wash cherry tomatoes and bell pepper. Remove seeds from pepper, and cut into cubes. Wash salad cucumber, cut in half, remove seeds, and cut into thick slices. Wash the radishes and cut into thick slices or cut in half (the vegetables should be similar in size).
- Stick the vegetables, mozzarella balls (perhaps cut in half), and basil leaves onto the skewer so there is an even number of mozzarella balls and tomatoes.
- Mix the balsamic vinegar, olive oil, and salt and put onto a flat plate.
- Apply the marinade to all sides of the vegetables and flavor with a few dashes of rose hydrolate spray. Serve on dessert plates right away with toasted bread triangles.

TIP:
For the vegan variation, simply leave out the mozzarella balls or replace with slices of tofu.

TIP:
It is easier to place the pieces onto the skewers if you soak them for 20 minutes before use.

Warm Appetizers and Soups

All recipes are for 4 portions

Mushroom Spring Roll

INGREDIENTS

FILLING

½ lb	mushrooms (porcini, shitake, button, etc.)
1	shallot or 1 small onion
1 tbsp	oil
1 drp	garlic oil
1 drp	thyme oil ct.* linalool
1 tsp	olive paste
•	salt and pepper

- Rice paper leaves or strudel pastry leaves
- 1 egg white or water to brush
- sufficient oil and clarified butter for baking

* "ct." stands for chemotype. There are other chemotypes of thyme oil, however, they are not apt for use in the kitchen. Make sure you read the label (see explanation on page 9).

PREPARATION TIME: 45 min. • **DIFFICULTY:** Elaborate

- Cut mushrooms into cubes; finely chop shallot or onion and fry in a pan without oil with the mushrooms. Leave to cool, then add the essential oils emulsified with the olive paste. Season with salt and pepper.

VARIATION:

Strudel Pastry Baskets with Mushroom Filling

- Strudel pastry baskets are fried in hot oil (coconut oil), using a fairly tall pot (diameter 8", height 5–6"). Heat coconut oil to 350-400º F.
- Use a thick cork (diameter 1½", height 1") stuck onto a knitting needle. Place a piece of pastry over it and dip briefly into the hot fat to fry. Fill the pastry baskets and serve.

- Place the filling onto the rice or strudel pastry leaves brushed with water or beaten egg white; roll up, and fry the rolls in the oil–clarified butter mix.

Orange Dates with Bacon

INGREDIENTS

16 dates
  • orange sugar
16 slices of bacon

16 toothpicks

PREPARATION TIME: 20 min.   •   **DIFFICULTY:** Easy

• Remove the pits from the dates and fill with a knife tip´s quantity of orange sugar.
• Wrap the dates with a slice of bacon.
• Fry the bacon in a pan without oil until it is crunchy. Place dates on toothpicks, serve warm.

VEGAN VARIATION:

• Wrap orange dates with thin zucchini slices and fry in a pan with 2 tbsp of olive oil.

TIP:
You can prepare this appetizer ahead of time and warm it up for 10 minutes in the oven at 200° F before serving.

Spaghetti with Shrimp Sauce

1 lb spaghetti

SAUCE

1 small onion
1 tbsp olive oil
½ lb shrimp
½ C fish stock
1 C cream
1 tsp lemon oil
(see page 32)
1 drp cilantroseed oil
½ tsp paprika
½ dried chili pepper

PREPARATION TIME: 15 min. • **DIFFICULTY:** Easy

- Boil spaghetti in salted water until "al dente."
- Finely chop onion and fry in hot olive oil; add shrimp, stirring frequently until shrimp is cooked.
- Deglaze pan with fish stock and add cream. Season with lemon oil and cilantroseed oil, paprika, and finely chopped chili pepper.
- Mix the sauce with the drained spaghetti and serve.

Noodles with Zucchini Cream Sauce

INGREDIENTS

1 lb spaghetti or ribbon noodles
1 thick slice of bacon
1 tbsp oil
1 small onion
1 garlic clove
1 drp thyme oil ct. linalool
(see explanation on page 62)
1 tbsp cream
2 small zucchini, shredded
1 sprig of thyme
• cream cheese

PREPARATION TIME: 20 min. • **DIFFICULTY:** Easy

- Cook noodles in salted water until "al dente."
- Cut the bacon into small cubes and fry in a little oil. Chop the onion and the garlic and briefly saute with the rest.
- Emulsify a drop of thyme oil with cream and pour into the bacon-garlic-onion mix.
- Add the shredded zucchini and the thyme sprig and simmer for a minute or two.
- Add cheese and stir until the sauce has a smooth consistency.
- Mix with drained spaghetti or ribbon noodles and serve.

Indian Meatballs with Aromatic Sauce

MEATBALLS

1	large onion
2 lb	ground meat mixture
1	egg
1 tsp	sea salt
1 tsp	cilantro oil
1 tsp	cumin powder
½ tsp	cardamom powder
1–2 tbsp	breadcrumbs
•	cold-pressed organic sesame hoil for frying

SAUCE

1 C	sour cream
1	knife tip of blood orange–lemon-grass salt (see page 34)
•	fresh mint leaves or ½ drp mint oil

PREPARATION TIME: 45 min. • **WAITING TIME:** 4 hours • **DIFFICULTY:** Elaborate

• For the sauce, mix the sour cream with blood orange–lemongrass salt and finely chopped peppermint leaves or ½ drop mint oil using the spoon method. Allow to soak for at least 4 hours.

• For the meatballs, finely chop the onion. Mix the ground meat with egg, onion and spices, adding sufficient breadcrumbs to achieve a smooth mixture that can be shaped.

• Using a teaspoon to scoop the ground meat, shape small balls with wet hands.

• Fry these balls on all sides in cold-pressed sesame oil. Serve the meatballs with the sauce while warm.

TIP:
You can prepare the meatballs the day before and store in the fridge. Before serving, heat them for 15–20 minutes at 225° F in the oven and serve with the sauce.

Zucchini Wafers (vegetarian)

INGREDIENTS

¾ lb zucchini
1 egg
½ drp tarragon oil
(spoon method;
see page 21)
2 drp garlic oil
1 tbsp chopped tarragon
⅔ C flour
1 C semolina or
breadcrumbs
• salt, pepper
• oil or clarified butter
for frying

PREPARATION TIME: 20 min. • **WAITING TIME:** 15 min. • **DIFFICULTY:** Easy

• Grate zucchini, add a pinch of salt and leave for a few minutes, then squeeze out water.
• Mix the zucchini with the egg, the essential oil, chopped tarragon, flour, and semolina. Add salt and pepper, and leave for 15 minutes.
• Shape patties with your wet hands and, in a skillet, fry in hot oil or clarified butter on both sides.

TIP:
A good choice: serve with tomato sauce or a simple garlic dip.

Carrot Soup with Lime Oil and Smoked Trout

INGREDIENTS

¾ lb carrots
½ onion or 3 shallots
3 tbsp olive oil
½ chili pepper
½ C white wine
1 C chicken or
vegetable stock
2 drp garlic oil
½ drp thyme oil
(spoon method;
see page 21)
½ drp rosemary oil
(spoon method;
see page 21)
1 drp vanilla extract
1 C coconut milk
• salt, pepper
3 tbsp butter
½ C cream
1 drp lime oil
5 oz smoked trout

PREPARATION TIME: 45 min. • **DIFFICULTY:** Easy

• Wash and peel carrots and cut into slices. Peel onion and shallots and chop into cubes. Heat olive oil, braise shallots and carrot slices, then add the finely chopped chili pepper.
• Deglaze pan with white wine and add the chicken or vegetable stock. Boil the carrots and shallots in it until tender, then blend into a smooth consistency.
• Emulsify the garlic, thyme and rosemary oils as well as the vanilla extract with the coconut milk. Blend with the soup; season with salt and pepper.

• Just before serving, add the cold butter to the soup and stir.
Whip cream until stiff, adding 1 drp of lime oil. Garnish the soup with the cream and add the smoked fish.

TIP:
Croutons are a great choice for this soup.

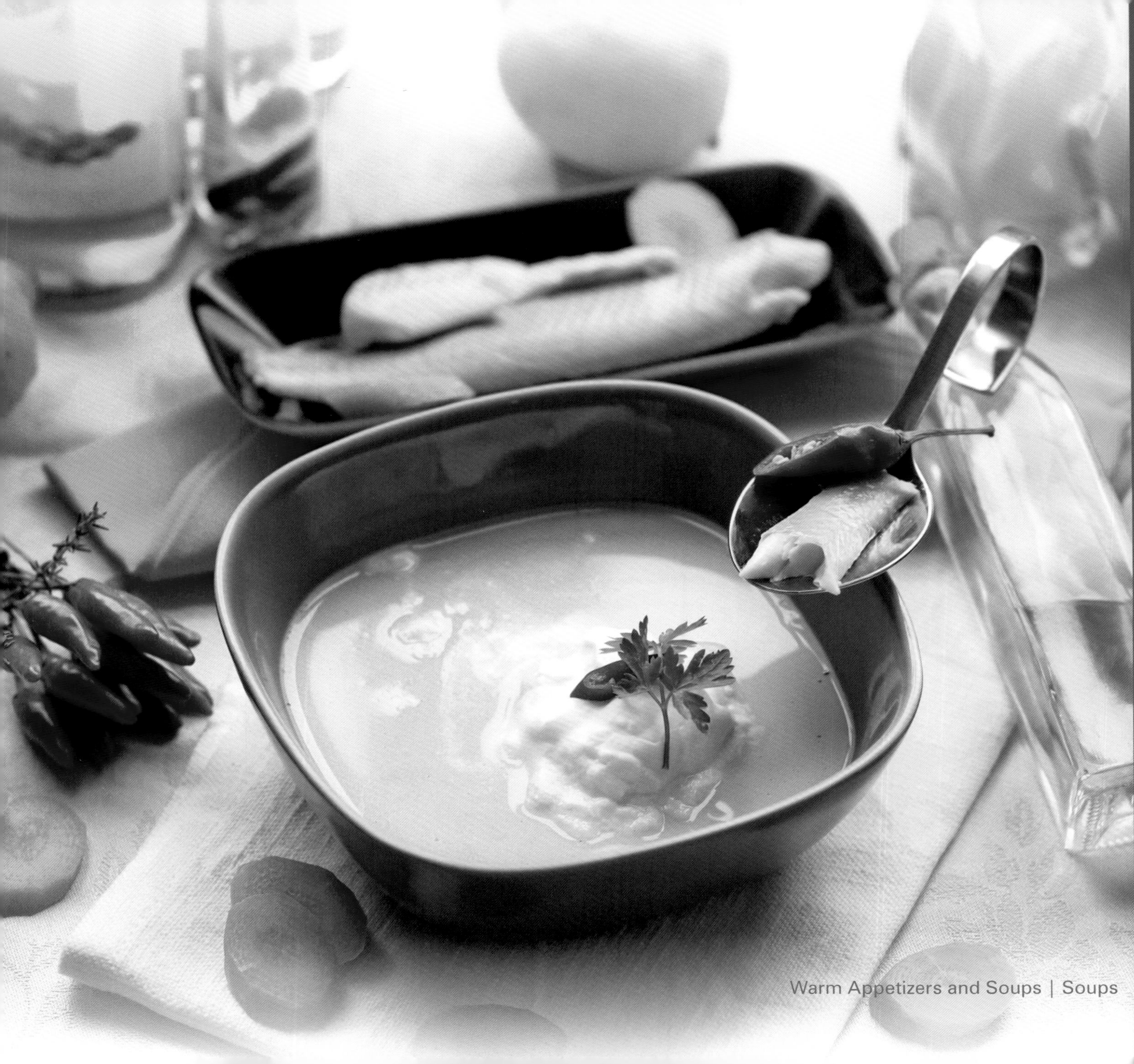

Pumpkin-Apple Soup

1 lb pumpkin or other
winter squash
(e.g., butternut,
hokkaido or musquee)
1 small onion
1 tbsp butter
1 tbsp organic coconut oil
1 apple
½ C dry white wine
¼ C calvados
3 C vegetable stock
1 pinch salt
1 pinch pepper
2 tbsp crème fraîche
or sour cream
1 tsp cornstarch
½ C cream
½ drp thyme oil
(spoon method;
see page 21)
½ drp rosemary oil
(spoon method;
see page 21)
2 drp nutmeg oil

PREPARATION TIME: 20 min. • **COOKING TIME:** Approx. 30 min.
DIFFICULTY: Easy

• Peel the pumpkin and cut into small pieces. Finely chop onion and braise in butter and coconut oil until glassy.
• Add the pumpkin pieces and the peeled apple and briefly fry with the rest.
• Deglaze pan with white wine and calvados; add the vegetable stock and season. Leave to boil until pumpkin and apple are soft.

• Mix crème fraîche with the cornstarch and add to the soup. Emulsify the essential oil and a small amount of soup, add to the soup and blend, then strain with a sieve and serve hot.

TIP:
This soup is particularly tasty with a few drops of pumpkin seed oil and braised apple slices flavored with vanilla oil.

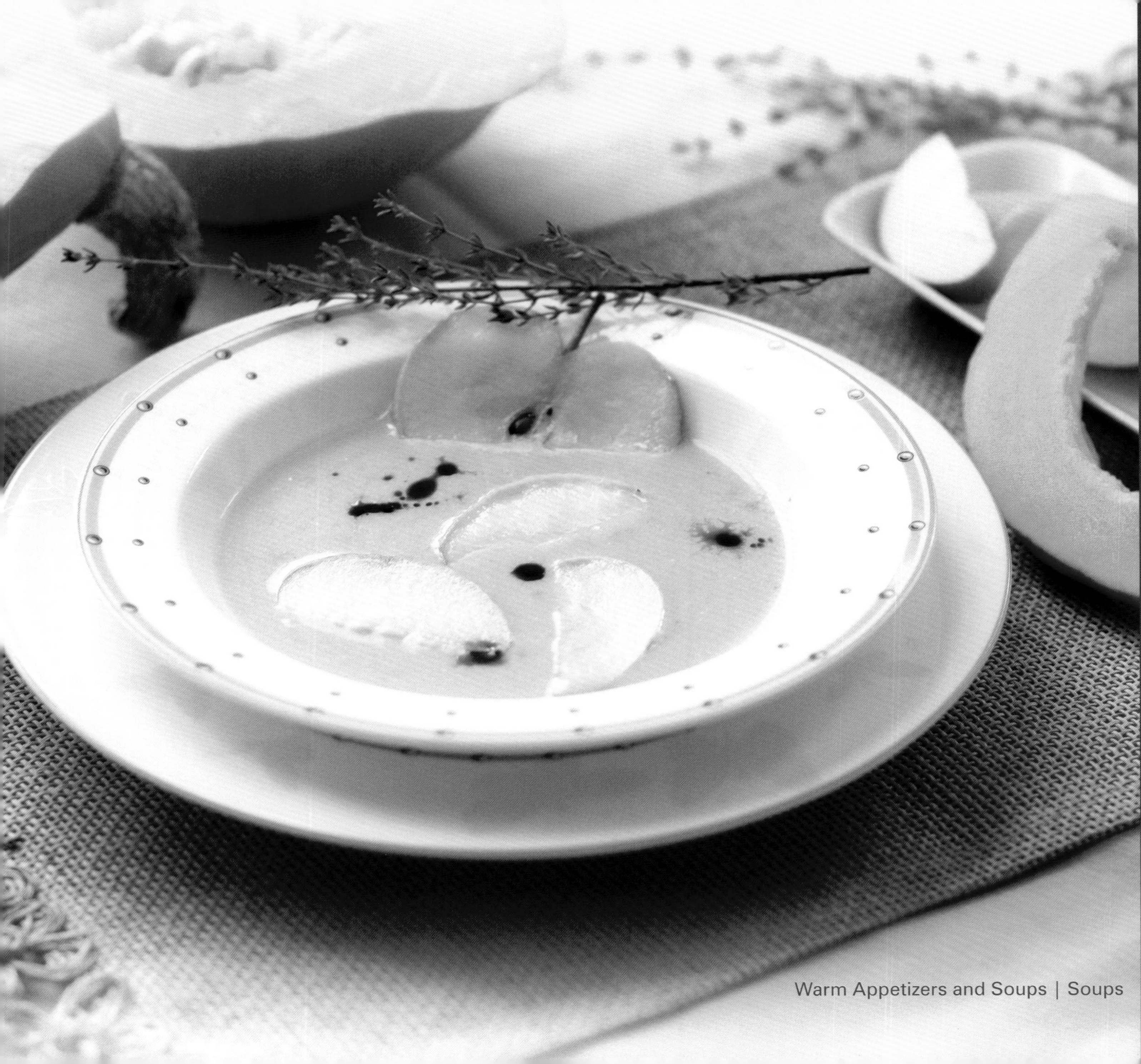

Pumpkin Soup

PREPARATION TIME: 20 min. • **COOKING TIME:** Approx. 35 min. • **DIFFICULTY:** Medium

INGREDIENTS

1 lb	pumplin (or other winter squash, e.g., butternut, hokkaido, musquee)
2	medium-sized onions
2–3 tbsp	olive oil
•	water or vegetable broth
•	a few saffron threads
¾ C	crème fraîche
2 drp	cilantroseed oil
1 drp	ginger oil, CO₂-extracted (see page 11)
1 pinch	sea salt

• After washing, cut the pumpkin in half; and remove seeds. Cut into cubes with the skin on (this adds a more intense color), removing any bad sections and spots.

• Finely chop the onion. Gently heat the olive oil in a pot and braise the onion until it is golden (the olive oil must never get too hot!). Add the pumpkin cubes and as much water or vegetable stock needed to barely cover them.

• Shred the saffron threads and add them. Boil gently until the pumpkin cubes are soft, then mash to a fine consistency. Bring to a boil once more (if it is too thick, add water or vegetable broth).

• Meanwhile, emulsify the crème fraîche with the essential oils. Take the pot with the hot soup off the heat and mix in the crème fraîche–oil mix with a whisk. Season with sea salt and serve immediately in soup bowls.

TIP:
You can refine the soup with 1 tsp of whipped cream and a few drops of pumpkin oil.

TIP:
For the vegan variation, use soy milk instead of crème fraîche: mix 3–4 tbsp soy milk with the essential oils and mix with a whisk.

TIP:
This soup can easily be prepared the day before, except for making and adding bthe crème fraîche–oil mix.

Cold Cucumber Soup with Cilantroseed Oil

INGREDIENTS

2	salad cucumbers
1 pinch	sea salt
1 pinch	pepper
3 tbsp	finely chopped dill
2 C	sour cream
3–5 drp	cilantroseed oil
1 tbsp	olive oil
½ C	whipped cream
•	fresh dill for garnishing

PREPARATION TIME: 20 min. • **WAITING TIME:** 2–3 hours • **DIFFICULTY:** Easy

• Peel cucumbers, cut in half, and remove seeds; cut into small pieces. Then mash the cucumber pieces.
• Add sea salt, pepper, dill, and sour cream and mix again. Refrigerate for several hours.

• Take from the refrigerator 30 minutes before serving; emulsify the cilantroseed oil with the olive oil and mix into the soup with a whisk.
• Serve with whipped cream and dill in soup bowls.

Riesling Soup with Cinnamon Oil

INGREDIENTS

2	medium-sized onions
4 tbsp	butter
2 C	Riesling
2 C	beef broth
2/3 C	crème fraîche
1 drp	cinnamon oil, Ceylon quality, CO_2 -extracted (see page 11)
1 pinch	ground nutmeg
1 pinch	sea salt
1 pinch	white pepper

PREPARATION TIME: 15 min. • **COOKING TIME:** Approx. 20 min. • **DIFFICULTY:** Easy

• Peel the onions and dice. Melt the butter and braise the onions until golden.
• Deglaze the pan with Riesling and add the beef broth. Bring to a boil and simmer for another 15–20 minutes.
• Meanwhile, mix the crème fraîche with the cinnamon oil and the ground nutmeg.
• Remove the pan from the heat. Mix the crème fraîche into the soup with a whisk, season with sea salt and pepper, blend with an immersion blender, and serve right away in soup bowls.

TIP:
You can serve the soup with whipped cream or garnished with croutons.

TIP:
For a simple vegan variation, just use 3–4 tbsp of soy milk instead of crème fraîche (see also the tip on page 74).

Indian Tomato Soup

PREPARATION TIME: 20 min. • COOKING TIME: 20 min. • DIFFICULTY: Medium

INGREDIENTS

2	medium-sized onions
2	small garlic cloves
3 tbsp	coconut oil
1	dried chili pepper (optional)
1 tsp	cumin powder
1 C	coconut milk
24 oz	crushed tomatoes (from a can)
4 drp	cilantroseed oil
2 drp	cardamom oil
1 drp	cinnamon bark oil, CO_2-extracted (see page 11)
1 pinch	sea salt
•	a few fresh mint leaves for garnishing

• Peel and finely chop onions and garlic. Heat the coconut oil in a pot and braise the onions until they are golden. Add the garlic (and, if desired, the chili pepper) and fry briefly, otherwise the garlic might turn bitter.

• Remove the pot from the heat and add cumin. Set 2 tbsp of coconut milk aside. Use the remaining coconut milk to deglaze the onion-garlic mix and return the pot to the stove.

• Add the crushed tomatoes while stirring. Simmer gently for 20 minutes. If you added the whole chili pepper, remove it now.

• Use the immersion blender to make a smooth soup. Remove the pot from the heat. Emulsify the essential oils with the 2 tbsp of coconut milk and season the soup with it.

• Season the soup with sea salt, garnish with finely chopped mint leaves, and serve in soup bowls.

TIP:

In case your guests would enjoy their soup spicier, offer them the chili spice oil. With 1–2 drops they can season the soup as they wish!

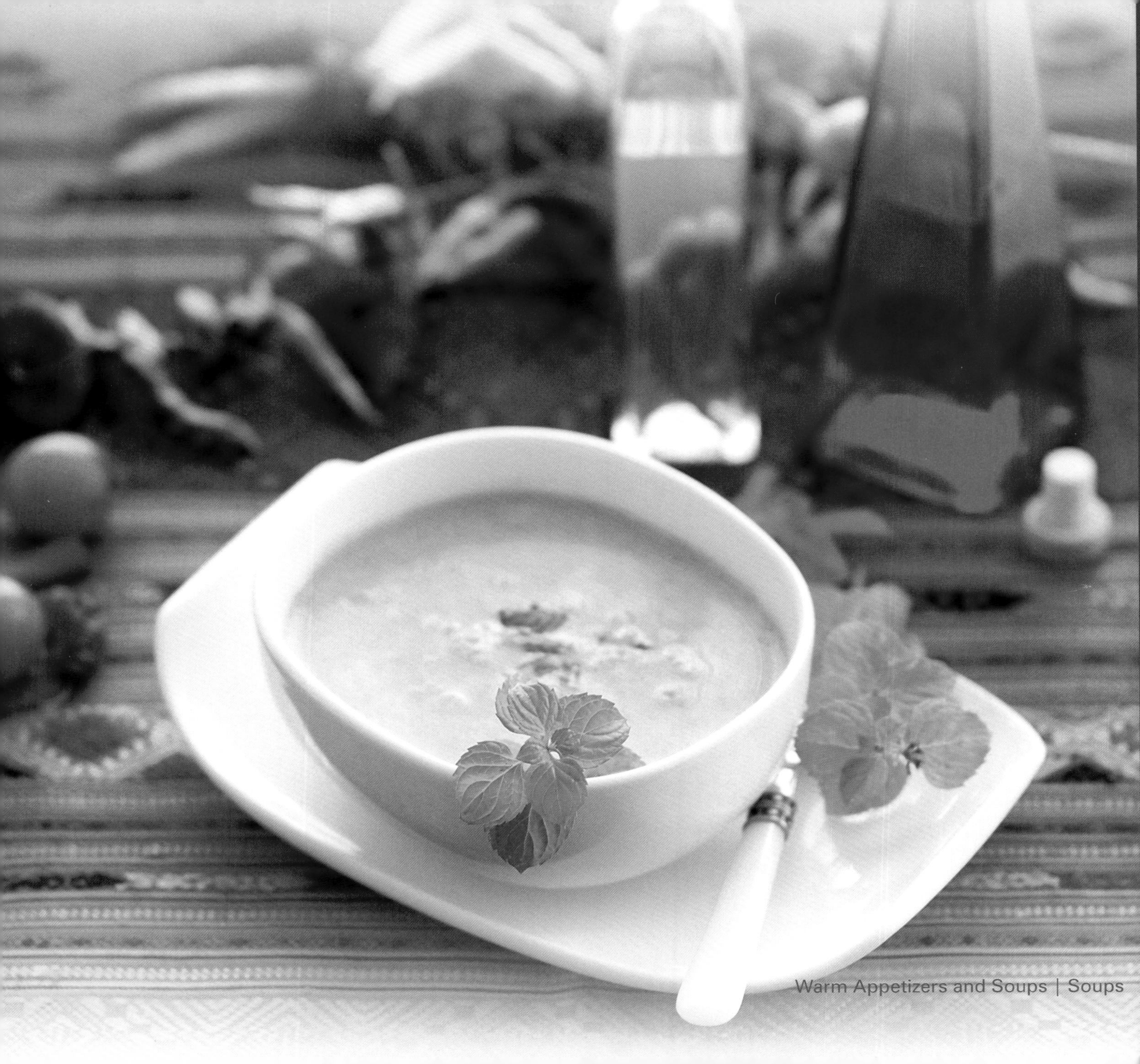

Tomato-Fennel Soup

INGREDIENTS

1	onion
1	garlic clove
1 tbsp	olive oil
1	fennel bulb
1 lb	ripe tomatoes
3-4	saffron threads
1	sprinkle of tomato vinegar
½ C	white wine
2 C	vegetable stock
1 tsp	sugar
1 pinch	salt
1	sprinkle of Tabasco (optional)
1 drp	sweet fennel oil
3 drp	black pepper oil
½ C	cream

• Chop onion and garlic and braise in olive oil. Add fennel cut into slices, diced tomatoes, and saffron threads, and fry.

• Deglaze the pan with vinegar and white wine and add vegetable stock. Boil for 30 minutes.

• Blend the soup, strain it, and season with sugar, salt, and, if desired, Tabasco.

• Emulsify the pepper oil with the cream and add to the soup.

TIP:
You can also add thinly sliced dried tomatoes to this soup.

Cauliflower Soup with Coconut Milk and Ginger Oil

INGREDIENTS

1 lb cauliflower
2 lemon slices
1 bay leaf
½ C broth or vegetable stock
2 C coconut milk
¾ C crème fraîche
2 drp ginger oil (see page 10)
1 drp ginger oil, CO_2-extracted (see page 11)
1–2 tsp curry powder
1 pinch sea salt

PREPARATION TIME: 20 min. • **COOKING TIME:** 15–20 min. • **DIFFICULTY:** Medium

• Remove the leaves from the cauliflower and divide into small florets. Boil with the lemon slices and the laurel leaf until soft. As soon as the cauliflower is soft, remove it and set the broth aside.
• Blend the cauliflower florets with the broth or the vegetable stock and the coconut milk and fill a second pot with it. If the soup is too thick, add more broth or stock and briefly boil.
• Remove the pot from the heat. Mix the crème fraîche with the essential oils and the curry powder and add to the soup with a whisk.

• Season with sea salt and serve in soup bowls or cups.

TIP:

To garnish, whip a half-cup of cream with 1-2 drops black pepper essential oil and place one spoonful each serving of the soup.

TIP:

If you invited your guests for a several-course menu, it makes sense to prepare a few things the day before. Except for the addition of the crème fraîche, this soup can be prepared the day before. Keep it in the fridge overnight, briefly boil before seasoning, and serve with the crème fraîche–spice oil mix.

TIP:

For the vegan variation simply use soy milk instead of crème fraîche. Mix 3–4 tbsp with the curry powder and the essential oils and blend with a whisk.

Mango Soup with Lemongrass and Cinnamon Oil

PREPARATION TIME: 20 min. • **COOKING TIME:** 15-20 min. • **DIFFICULTY:** Medium

INGREDIENTS

2	ripe mangoes
1	medium-sized onion
2	small garlic cloves
2 tbsp	butter
½ C	white wine
1 qt	beef or vegetable stock
1	chili pepper
4 tbsp	whipped cream or 1 tbsp crème fraîche
1–2 drp	lemongrass oil
1–2 drp	cilantroseed oil
1 drp	cinnamon oil, CO₂-extracted (see page 11)
1 pinch	sea salt
1 pinch	white pepper

• Peel the mangoes, cut the pulp from the pit, and cut into cubes.

• Peel the onion and the garlic and chop. Heat the butter in a pot and braise the onions until golden; add the garlic and saute briefly.

• Add the mango cubes and braise for a few minutes. Deglaze the pan with white wine, add to the beef or vegetable stock, then add the whole chili pepper. Simmer for 15–20 minutes, then remove the chili pepper and blend the soup.

• Bring soup to a boil once more, then remove from the heat.

• Mix the cream or crème fraîche with the essential oils and add to the soup with a whisk.

• Season with salt and pepper and serve right away in soup bowls.

TIP:
It looks really nice if you sprinkle a few ground red peppercorns over the soup.

TIP:
You can prepare this soup the day before, except for the cream and oil mix.

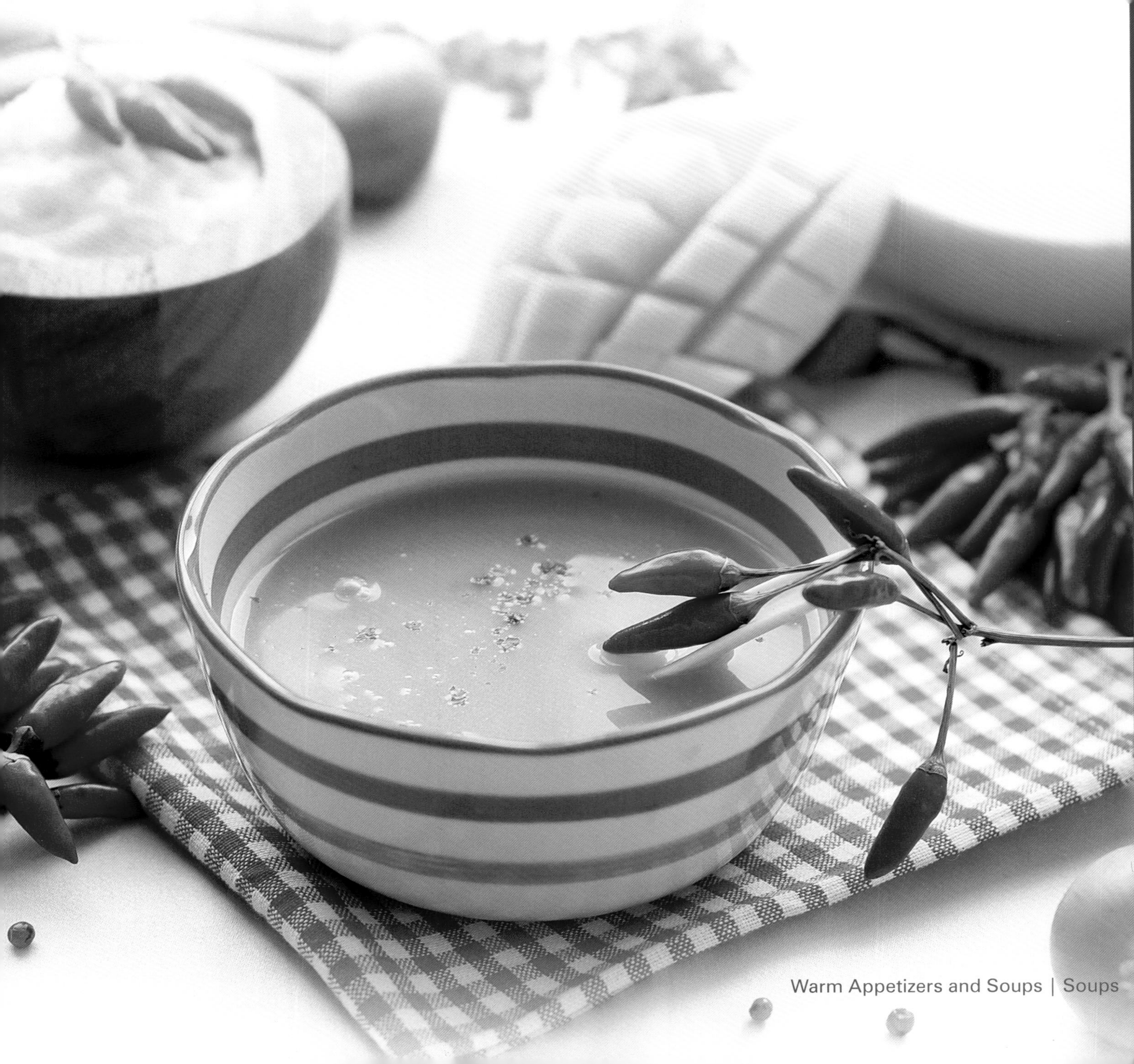

Zucchini Cream Soup with Lemongrass Oil & Scampi Skewers

INGREDIENTS

1	small onion
1	garlic clove
2 tbsp	coconut oil
1	large zucchini, sliced
2 C	vegetable stock
1 drp	lemongrass oil
2 drp	cilantroseed oil
1 C	coconut milk
6 oz	shrimp

PREPARATION TIME: 15 min.   •   **COOKING TIME:** Approx. 15 min.   •   **DIFFICULTY:** Easy

- Cut the onion into very thin rings and fry with the finely chopped garlic in coconut oil.
- Add the sliced zucchini and briefly saute.
- Add the vegetable stock, bring it to a boil, then blend.
- Emulsify the oils with the coconut milk and mix into the zucchini soup.
- Briefly fry the shrimp in hot oil, place on skewers, and serve with the soup.

TIP:
For a vegan variation, skip the shrimp and serve with croutons or roasted pine nuts.

TIP:
Yellow zucchini or summer squash make for a beautiful color!

Main Dishes

All recipes are for 4 portions

3	garlic cloves
1½ lb	pork filet
1 tbsp	cloves
1 pinch	sea salt
1 pinch	pepper
3–4 tbsp	lemon seasoning oil (see page 32)
3–4 tbsp	olive oil
1 C	red wine to deglaze
1 C	beef stock
2 tsp	dark gravy thickener (or cornstarch)
½ C	cold water
3 drp	orange oil
1 drp	bay oil
•	salt to emulsify

POLENTA-COFFEE SOUFFLÉ
Ingredients and recipe
on page 118

MORE SIDE DISH TIPS:
- Red Cabbage
  (see page 114)
- Glazed Chestnuts
  (see page 112)
- Oven Potato with Flavored Cream
  (see page. 116)
- Oriental Carrot Rice
  (see page 114)

"Aristo" Pork Filet with Polenta-Coffee Soufflé

PREPARATION TIME: 45 min. • **COOKING TIME:** Approx. 15 min.
WAITING TIME: At least 4 hours • **DIFFICULTY:** Elaborate

- Peel and cut garlic into thin slices for larding. Lard the pork filet with garlic pieces and cloves. Season with sea salt and pepper, put into a casserole, and pour lemon seasoning oil over it. It is best to refrigerate overnight, or at least 4 hours.
- Heat the olive oil in an ovenproof pan or casserole and braise the pork filet on all sides. Deglaze with red wine and simmer to reduce.
- Add the beef stock and bake the pork filet for 15 minutes in a pre-heated oven at 350° F (the meat should still be slightly pink at the center).

- Remove the meat from the oven and let it rest for another 5 minutes, covered with aluminum foil.
- Meanwhile, prepare the sauce by mixing the gravy thickener with cold water. Add the essential oils emulsified with salt and simmer until the sauce has thickened.
- Cut the meat into thick slices and serve on warmed plates with a side dish or two. Pour sauce over it just before serving.

TIP:
You can round off the sauce with 2–3 tbsp of cream (mix the cream with the gravy thickener and the essential oils and use to thicken the sauce). Its color becomes lighter.

TIP:
A meat thermometer helps ensure the right cooking temperature!
Core temperature for pork: 160° F (medium).
Core temperature for venison or beef: 140–150° F (medium).

Roasted Venison Filet with Red Cabbage

PREPARATION TIME: 20 min. • **COOKING TIME:** Approx. 20 min.
WAITING TIME: Approx. 6 hours. • **DIFFICULTY:** Medium

INGREDIENTS

- 1½ lb   venison filet
- 1 pinch   salt
- 1 pinch   pepper
- 1 tsp   butter
- •   some broth
- 1 tbsp   cornstarch

MARINADE

- ½ C   olive oil
- 2 drp   laurel oil
- 1 drp   juniper oil
- 1 drp   thyme oil ct. linalool
        (see page 62)
- 1 drp   essential orange and
        lemon oil

RED CABBAGE

Ingredients and recipe
on page 114

ADDITIONAL TIPS FOR SIDE DISHES:

- *Baby Potatoes with Minted Butter
  (see page 122)*
- *Pumpkin Gnocchi (see page 108)*

• Prepare a marinade from the olive oil and essential oils and marinate the venison filet for 6 hours. Remove from the marinade (keep it) and add salt and pepper to the meat.
• Heat an ovenproof pan or casserole on the stove and braise the filet on all sides over high heat.
• Cook the meat in a pre-heated oven at 325° F for about 15–20 minutes. Remove the meat, cover with aluminum foil, and let it rest.
• Pour off the fat from the pan or casserole, and place the pan on the stovetop. Put the butter in the pan and add the marinade.

• Add some and bring to a boil; mix in cornstarch with a whisk to thicken the sauce, and bring to a boil once more.
• Cut the meat into portions and serve with the sauce and the red cabbage.

TIP:
This recipe is also suited for duck breast: cut the skin of the duck breasts in a cross pattern, marinate them as described, and add salt and pepper. Briefly fry the meat side and on the skin side a bit longer. Proceed as described for the venison filet.

4 beef filet medallions
(each about 1" thick)
1 tbsp pepper seasoning oil
(see page 30)
1 pinch pepper and salt, each
• some oil for frying
3½ tbsp butter
½ onion
• juice of ½ lemon
2 drp garlic oil
2 drp lemon orange oil
2 drp orange oil
1 tbsp Grand Marnier
2 tsp cognac
• orange

Beef Medallions with Orange-Pepper Sauce

PREPARATION TIME: 30 min. • **DIFFICULTY:** Medium

• Rub the medallions with pepper seasoning oil, pepper, and salt, and briefly saute on both sides.
• Add a walnut-sized piece of butter to the pan juices and braise the finely chopped onion. Deglaze the pan with the lemon juice and boil briefly.
• Add garlic oil, lemon oil, and orange oil. Season with Grand Marnier, cognac, and pepper seasoning oil.

• Peel the orange, cut into cubes, and add.
• Pour the sauce over the beef medallions and serve.

SIDE DISH TIP:
Tagliatelle pasta.

INGREDIENTS

4 chicken drumsticks
1 pinch salt
1 pinch pepper

MARINADE
• rosemary and thyme
1 sprig each
• some fennel
2–3 sage leaves
3 drp garlic, rosemary, and
sage oils, each
1 drp fennel oil
2 tbsp green olives
without pits
• some lemon juice
2 tbsp olive oil

Mediterranean Chicken Drumsticks

PREPARATION TIME: 15 min. • **COOKING TIME:** 40 min.
WAITING TIME: 4 hours • **DIFFICULTY:** Easy

• Wash and dry the chicken drumsticks. Mix together all of the ingredients for the marinade.
• Pour the marinade over the chicken drumsticks and let marinate for at least 4 hours, turning occasionally.
• Heat the oven to 400–450°F. Add salt and pepper, and fry in a pan for about

40 minutes, turning frequently. Add the remaining marinade to the resulting broth.

SIDE DISH TIPS:
• *Baby Potatoes with Mint Butter (see page 122)*
• *Rice*

Asian Chicken Drumsticks with Couscous Salad

INGREDIENTS

4	chicken drumsticks
1 pinch	salt
1 pinch	pepper

MARINADE

1	piece of ginger (1½")
1	garlic clove
1	chili pepper
	juice of ½ lime
	or ½ lemon
1 tsp	honey
2 drp	garlic oil
4 drp	cilantroseed oil
1 drp	ginger oil
2 drp	lemon or lime oil
2 tbsp	sesame oil
2 tbsp	sunflower oil

COUSCOUS SALAD
Ingredients and recipe
on page 50

SIDE DISH TIP:
Basmati rice

PREPARATION TIME: 15 min. • **COOKING TIME:** 40 min.
WAITING TIME: 4 hours • **DIFFICULTY:** Easy

• Wash chicken drumsticks and dry. To prepare the marinade, peel the ginger and garlic and remove seeds from the chili pepper.
• Mix the lime or lemon juice with the honey and the essential oils. Add the finely chopped garlic, ginger, and chili pepper, as well as the sesame and sunflower oil.
• Spread the marinade over the chicken and leave for at least 4 hours, turning the drumsticks over occasionally.

• Heat oven to 400–425° F. Remove chicken from the marinade, add salt and pepper, and roast for about 40 minutes; turning frequently. Add some of the marinade to the resulting broth.
• Serve with couscous salad and garnish with pomegranate seeds.

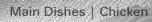

Tajine Chicken with Lemon and Artichoke Hearts

PREPARATION TIME: 20 min. • **COOKING TIME:** Approx. 60 min. • **DIFFICULTY:** Medium

INGREDIENTS

1	chicken (approx. 3 lbs)
2 tbsp	butter
2 tbsp	native olive oil
1 pinch	ginger salt
1 pinch	black pepper
1	small piece of ginger
1	onion
8	saffron threads, ground
10	stalks of parsley
1 C	chicken broth
1	untreated lemon
1 tbsp	cilantro spice oil (see page 30)
½ tbsp	ginger spice oil (see page 30)
½ tbsp	cumin spice oil (see page 30)
2 drp	lemon seasoning oil (see page 32)
2	artichoke hearts (canned)

• Cut the chicken into pieces. Heat butter and olive oil in a pan. Fry the chicken, seasoning with ginger salt, pepper, and the finely chopped ginger.
• Add the finely chopped onion, the saffron threads, and the parsley. Add soup and put everything into a pot or a tajine. Close the top and leave in the oven for 50–60 minutes at 400° F, until the chicken is soft.
• Remove the meat from the tajine and keep warm. Boil the sauce in a pot (remove the parsley stalks first), add the lemon peel (cut into thin strips), and season with the spice oils.

• Serve the chicken with the sauce and garnish with halved artichoke hearts.

NOTE:
If you use a clay cooker or a clay tajine, soak both parts for 30 minutes in water prior to use, and place into the cold oven. The cooking time takes a little longer. If you are using a glazed tajine, preheat the oven.

Chicken Satay Sticks with Oriental Carrot Rice

INGREDIENTS

4 chicken breasts

MARINADE
2 drp thyme oil ct. linalool
       (see page 62)
1 drp rosemary oil
1 drp orange oil
½ C buttermilk or yogurt

wooden skewers or
rosemary sprigs

ORIENTAL CARROT RICE
Ingredients and recipe
on page 114

PREPARATION TIME: 15 min. • **COOKING TIME:** 30 min. • **DIFFICULTY:** Easy

• Cut the chicken breasts into thin strips. Emulsify the essential oils with buttermilk or yogurt, and marinate the chicken for at least 30 minutes.
• Stick the marinated pieces onto the skewers or the rosemary twigs and grill on both sides or fry in a pan.

SIDE DISH TIP:
Summer Vegetables with Vanilla and Garlic (see page 120)

"Citronnier" Salmon with Summer Vegetables

INGREDIENTS

	• zest of 1 lemon (untreated)
2-3 tbsp	lemon spice oil (see page 32)
4	salmon filets
1 pinch	sea salt
1 pinch	pepper
	• fresh lemon thyme
	• fresh marjoram
1 pinch	blood orange–lemongrass salt (see page 34)
4 pcs	aluminum foil or 1 casserole

SUMMER VEGETABLES WITH VANILLA AND GARLIC
Ingredients and recipe on page 120

PREPARATION TIME: 15 min. • **COOKING TIME:** 25 min. • **DIFFICULTY:** Easy

• Drip lemon seasoning oil on the lemon zest and set aside. Salt the salmon slightly, then add pepper, lemon thyme, and marjoram.
• Cook the salmon filets wrapped in aluminum foil or in a covered casserole at 300° F for 25 minutes.
• Serve the salmon filets on pre-warmed plates. Season with the orange–lemongrass salt, and add the prepared zest. Serve with summer vegetables.

SIDE DISH TIPS:
• *Basmati rice*
• *Warm Herb Baguette (see page 118)*
• *Leaf Salad with Orange Vinaigrette (see page. 51)*
• *Baby Potatoes with Mint Butter (see page 122)*

TIP:
You can use trout instead of salmon. Instead of baking in aluminum foil, fry the trout in a pan.

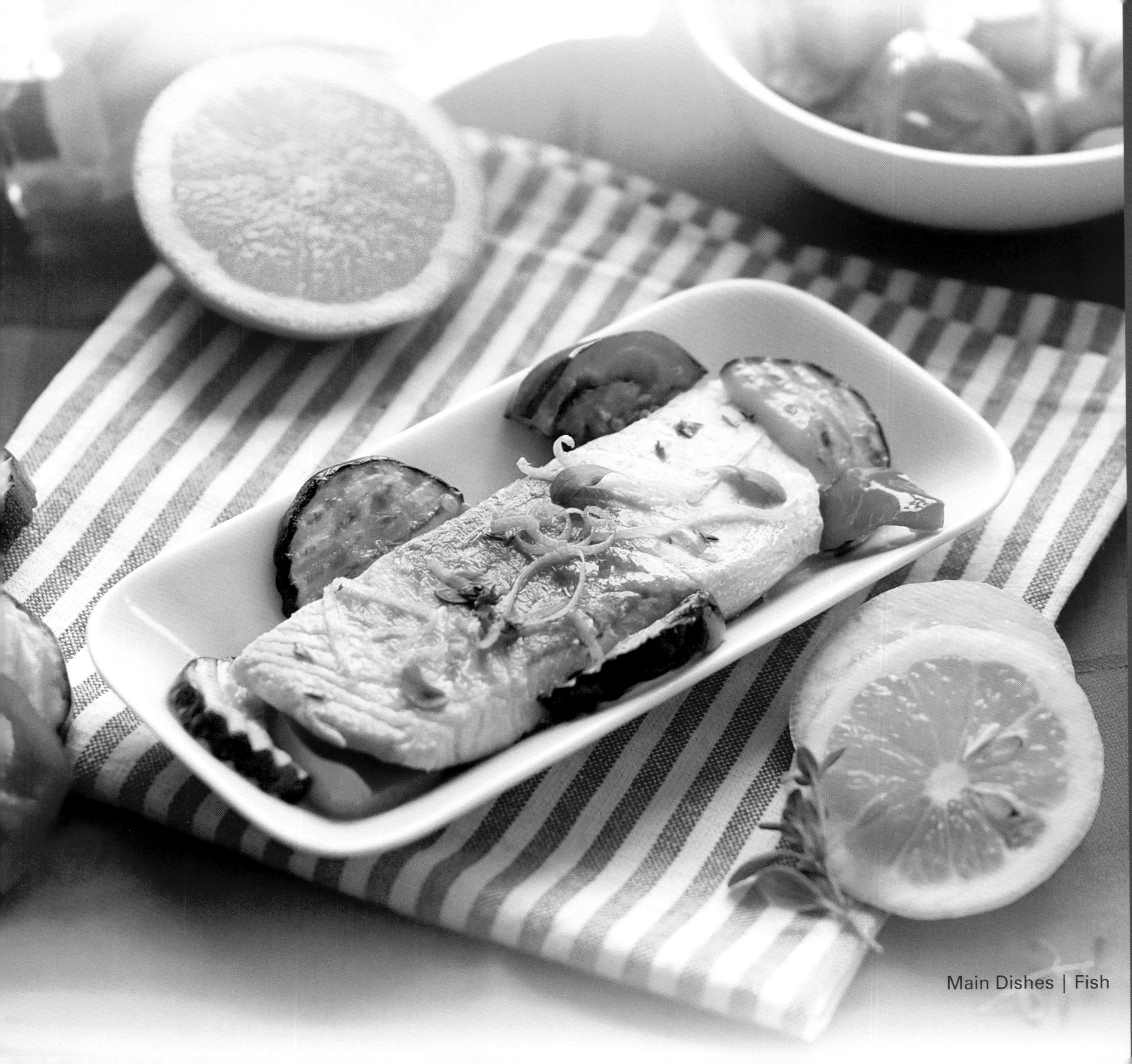

Coquilles St.-James with Sliced Vegetables

INGREDIENTS

1 bunch   spring onions or
           1 medium-sized onion
¼ lb   each of celery, carrots
       and leeks
3 tbsp   butter
        • a few saffron threads
3 C   vegetable broth
1½ lb   cleaned scallops
       (frozen or fresh)
½ C   whipped cream
        • juice and zest of
       1 orange
1 tsp   blood orange–
       lemongrass salt
       (see page 34)
1 pinch   pepper

PREPARATION TIME: 25 min. • **COOKING TIME:** Approx. 30 min. • **DIFFICULTY:** Medium

• Chop the spring onions. Wash the other vegetables and cut into fine strips or grate them.
• Heat the butter in a casserole and fry the spring onions until they are golden. Add the vegetables and saffron threads, soak for 5 minutes, then fry until the vegetables are glassy.
• Add the vegetable broth and boil for 5–7 minutes.
• Add the scallops and cook, covered, for another 15–20 minutes over medium heat.
• Add the cream and the orange juice and season with the spiced salt and pepper.
• Place on preheated plates; garnish with orange zest and serve immediately.

TIP:
If this dish is prepared for adults you can use white wine instead of orange juice. Add the wine beforehand: deglaze the vegetables with ½ cup of white wine, then add the vegetable broth.

SIDE DISH TIPS:
• *Leaf Salad with Orange Vinaigrette (see page 51)*
• *Boiled Potatoes*
• *Basmati rice (flavor with blood orange–lemongrass salt after boiling)*
• *Baby Potatoes with Mint Butter (see page 122)*
• *Warm Herb Baguette (see page 118)*

Lake Trout Confit*

INGREDIENTS

> 4 lake trout filets
> 1 qt high-quality olive oil
> 10 drp laurel oil
> 15 drp lemon oil
> 1 pinch sea salt

* **Confit:** cooking in oil or fat at low temperature. The method is used for gentle cooking of fish. This is a delicious recipe!

PREPARATION TIME: 10 min. • **COOKING TIME:** 10 min. • **DIFFICULTY:** Easy

• Cut the trout filets into slices about two fingers wide and place into a casserole. Mix the olive oil with the essential oils and heat to 175° F (check with a thermometer). Pour it over the slices in the casserole and leave to cook for 10 minutes at max. 175° F.
• Take the finished filets from the oil and let drain. Serve with a side dish of your choice and with a slice of lemon.

SIDE DISH TIPS:
• *Warm Herb Baguette (see page 118)*
• *Summer Vegetables with Vanilla and Garlic (see page 120)*
• *Baby Potatoes with Mint Butter (see page 122)*
• *Leaf Salad with Orange Vinaigrette (see page 51)*

Lemon-Garlic Char

INGREDIENTS

> 4 large char filets
> 1 lemon
> 2 garlic cloves
> 4 large potatoes
> 1 tbsp tarragon

MARINADE
> ½ C olive oil
> 4 drp tarragon oil
> 4 drp lemon oil
> 6 drp garlic oil

PREPARATION TIME: 35 min. • **COOKING TIME:** 25 min.
WAITING TIME: 60 min. • **DIFFICULTY:** Easy

• Wash the fish filets and dry; remove any bones.
• Mix the olive oil with the essential oils for the marinade and cover the fish filets. Marinate for about 60 minutes.
• Cut the lemon into slices, lay them in a roasting pan, then place the filets on top. Add the finely chopped garlic and the marinade.

• Peel the raw potatoes, cut them into thin slices, and add to the roasting pan.
• Add the finely chopped tarragon, and roast in a preheated, 300° F oven until the fish is cooked.

Stuffed Char Roll with Bell Pepper Sauce

INGREDIENTS
4 char filets

FILLING
2 char filets
¼ lb crawfish (brined crawfish are perfect)
¼ C whipped cream
1 small chili pepper
1 drp cilantroseed oil
• salt, pepper

BELL PEPPER SAUCE
1 large onion or 2 shallots
4 red bell peppers
1½ tbsp butter
½ C white wine
1¼ C vegetable stock
1 drp thyme ct. linalool (see page 62)
½ drp clove oil (spoon method; see page 21)
2 drp juniper oil
3 drp laurel oil
¼ C whipped cream

PREPARATION TIME: 25 min. • **COOKING TIME:** c. 25 min. • **DIFFICULTY:** Elaborate

• Carefully remove the bones from the char filets. For the filling, remove skin from two of the filets and cut the flesh into pieces. Blend with the crawfish and the cream.
• Remove the seeds from the chili pepper and chop it finely. Add together with the cilantroseed oil to the crawfish-and-fish paste and season with salt and pepper.
• Place the remaining filets with the skin side down, add the filling, and roll them up.
• Wrap each roll into a piece of buttered aluminum foil. Cook at about 350° F for 20–25 minutes.
• Meanwhile, peel the onion or the shallot for the sauce and finely chop. Cut the bell peppers in half, remove seeds and internal walls, and cut into cubes.

• Melt butter in a pot and braise the onions or shallots until translucent. Add bell pepper and braise as well.
• Add the wine and reduce until there is almost no liquid left. Add the vegetable stock and boil for about 20 minutes.
• Blend the sauce and strain through a sieve. Emulsify the oils with the cream and mix with the sauce.
• Serve the rolls with the sauce and garnish with pomegranate seeds.

TIP:
The bell pepper sauce is also delicious when you use yellow bell pepper.

SIDE DISH TIP:
Rice

Catfish Filets in Prosecco-Dill Sauce

2 catfish filets
• salt and pepper

SAUCE

1 small shallot
2 tbsp butter
2 tsp dry vermouth
1½ tbsp Prosecco
¾ C fish or lobster stock
2 drp dill oil,
CO$_2$-extracted
(see page 11)
⅓ C whipped cream
1½ tbsp frozen butter
1 pinch salt
1 pinch pepper

PREPARATION TIME: 35 min. • **DIFFICULTY:** Easy

• Peel the shallots for the sauce and chop. Heat butter in a pot and braise the shallot without coloring it.
• Deglaze pan with the vermouth and reduce liquid. First add the Prosecco, then the fish or lobster stock, and reduce liquid by about ⅓; Strain through a fine sieve.
• Salt and pepper the catfish filets and put in a oven-proof dish. Add some of the Prosecco-shallot base sauce, and cover the form with buttered baking paper. Bake in preheated oven at about 350° F for about 10 minutes.

• Emulsify dill oil with the cream and mix with the remaining base sauce. Cut the cold butter into small pieces; use a whisk to mix into the sauce, and season with salt and pepper. Use an immersion blender to get a foamy consistency.
• Serve the sauce with the cooked catfish filet.

TIP:
Pre-boiled potatoes fried in a little butter are great with this dish.

TIP:
If you prepare the sauce with lobster stock you get a nice color contrast.

Asian Shrimp in the Wok

INGREDIENTS

- 1 red bell pepper
- 1 zucchini or
  1 green bell
  pepper
- 3 medium-sized
  carrots
- 1 piece of ginger root
  (about 2–3 inches)
- 2 small garlic cloves
- 4 tbsp native sesame oil
- 1 lb shrimp
- 6 oz bamboo shoots
  (canned)
- ¼ lb soy sprouts
  (optional)
- 1 C Indonesian soy
  sauce (e.g., ketjap
  manis—it is less salty
  than Japanese or
  Chinese soy sauce)
- 1–2 tbsp Asian spice syrup
  (see page 36)

PREPARATION TIME: 30 min. • **COOKING TIME:** 15 min. • **DIFFICULTY:** Medium

- Wash and clean the bell pepper, zucchini, and carrots, and cut into cubes or strips. Peel and mince the ginger. Peel and mince the garlic.
- Heat the sesame oil in a cast iron skillet with a high rim or in a wok. First, fry the ginger briefly, then add the shrimp and fry until the shrimp liquid is gone (do not let them brown).
- Add the garlic and briefly stir. Add the vegetables and stir until everything is heated thoroughly.
- Add the soy sauce, reduce heat, and leave for about 15 minutes to lightly braise.
- Remove the skillet form the heat. Season with Asian spice syrup and serve immediately in bowls.

TIP:
If you don´t like it too hot, simply leave out the ginger.

TIP:
You can replace the shrimp with meat (chicken or pork). Cut the meat into thin strips and make sure the meat does not overcook, but acquires a nice color. It is best to saute the meat first, then proceed as described above. The preparation time might be a little longer.

SIDE DISH TIP:
- *Basmati rice*
- *Chinese egg noodles*

Shrimp in Curry-Lemongrass Coconut Milk

PREPARATION TIME: 20 min. • **COOKING TIME:** Approx. 20 min. • **DIFFICULTY:** Easy

INGREDIENTS

- seasonal vegetables as desired (zucchini, green beans, broccoli, carrots, bell pepper, etc.)
- 1 piece of ginger root (about 2–3 inches)
- 1 lb shrimp
- 2–3 tbsp coconut oil
- 2 C coconut milk
- 1 pinch sea salt
- 1–2 tbsp curry powder
- 3 drp lemongrass oil

- Chop the vegetables into fine pieces and blanch them. Peel the ginger and mince it.
- Briefly fry the shrimp and the ginger in a pan with the coconut oil; add the vegetables.
- After setting 1 tbsp aside, add the coconut milk. Season with sea salt and curry powder, and simmer for 15–20 minutes until the vegetables are "al dente."
- Just before serving, emulsify the lemongrass oil with the reserved coconut milk and mix in. Season with salt.

TIP:

If you like it particularly hot you can add a whole chili pepper when simmering, or you can add a few drops of chili spice oil at the end.

TIP:

For a vegan variation simply skip the shrimp and replace with more vegetables.

SIDE DISH TIPS:

- *Basmati rice*
- *Chinese egg noodles*

Rose Pasta with Rose-Mint Pesto

INGREDIENTS

PASTA DOUGH
- 1½ C wheat flour
- 1¼ C semolina
- 1 tsp salt
- 1 handful of rose petals (untreated)
- 2 drp rose oil
- 4 eggs

ROSE-MINT PESTO
- 3 handfuls of rose petals
- 1 handful of apple mint leaves
- • sweet salt (see page 36)
- • some lemon juice
- ⅔ C almond oil or olive oil
- 1½ oz Brazil nuts or pine nuts
- 1½ oz Parmesan (or Edam) cheese

• Mix the flour, semolina, salt, and finely chopped rose flowers. Put into a bowl and make a depression in the center.
• Emulsify the rose oil with the eggs and pour into the depression of the flour. Use your hands to form a smooth, shiny dough. Wrap in plastic and refrigerate for 60 minutes.
• For the pesto, cut the rose petals and mint leaves into thin strips and mix with the sweet salt and the lemon juice.
• Process together with the oil and the Brazil nuts or pine nuts in a food processor (or use a powerful immersion blender).
• Mix with the finely grated Parmesan or Edam cheese. Keep warm.
• Roll out the pasta dough with a rolling pin and cut into about ¾-inch-wide noodles (or use a pasta machine).
• Boil the pasta in salted water until "al dente." Drain, and immediately mix with warm pesto, and serve.

TIP:
Usually you should calculate about 1½ cups of dry pasta as an appetizer serving and about 3 cups of pasta as a main dish serving. In the case of homemade fresh noodles which contain more moisture and are therefore heavier, measure by weight, allowing 3 ounces per person for appetizers and 5 ounces per person for main dishes.

Savoy Cabbage Rolls (vegan)

INGREDIENTS

1	head savoy cabbage

FILLING

2	large onions
2	green bell peppers
2	tomatoes (or diced canned tomatoes)
3 tbsp	olive oil
1½ C	sunflower seeds
1½ C	water
2 tbsp	Sicilian seasoning oil (see page 31)
1 pinch	sea salt
1 pinch	pepper

PREPARATION TIME: 35 min. • **COOKING TIME:** 30 min. • **DIFFICULTY:** Medium

• Remove the outer, soiled leaves from the cabbage. Separate the remaining leaves and wash. Blanch them in boiling salted water for 5 minutes, then carefully remove and shock in ice water.
• For the filling, peel the onions and finely chop; wash the bell peppers, remove seeds, and chop.
• Pour boiling water over the tomatoes. Remove the skins and seeds and dice the pulp.
• Braise the onions in olive oil until they are transparent.
• Finely chop the sunflower seeds and add to the onions. Add the bell pepper and diced tomato and braise. Deglaze the pan with water and fry for another 10 minutes. Add 1 tbsp of Sicilian seasoning oil, sea salt, and pepper.
• Spread each cabbage leaf with 1 tbsp of the filling and roll up the filled leaves. Grease a heat-resistant dish with the remaining Sicilian seasoning oil, place the rolls in the dish, and bake in a preheated 350° F oven for about 30 minutes.

TIP:
Simple boiled potatoes make for a nice side dish.

Pumpkin Gnocchi (vegan)

INGREDIENTS

1	hokkaido pumpkin (about 2 lb)
2 lbs	potatoes
1 tsp	sea salt
½ tsp	pepper-orange salt (see page 35)
•	some ground nutmeg
1½ C	spelt flour
5 tbsp	olive oil
2	sage leaves
1	handful of roasted almonds or pinenuts

• Clean the hokkaido pumpkin, cut in half, remove seeds, and cut into slices. Cook the slices in a preheated oven at 350° F for about 30 minutes.

• Meanwhile, boil the potatoes with about 1 tsp of sea salt and mash them.

• Mash the soft pumpkin slices and mix with the potatoes. Season with pepper-orange salt and nutmeg, and add only enough flour to make the dough non-sticky.

• Roll the dough into ropes and cut into small pieces (gnocchi).

• Boil the gnocchi in salted water until they float to the surface. Carefully remove them with a slotted spoon.

• Gently heat the olive oil in a pan and braise the chopped sage leaves briefly. Add the gnocchi and stir.

• Serve the gnocchi immediately with roasted almonds or pinenuts.

VARIATION:
You can also serve the gnocchi with leaf spinach. Use fresh leaf spinach instead of the sage leaves in the olive oil, add the gnocchi, stir briefly, and serve with roasted almonds or pinenuts.

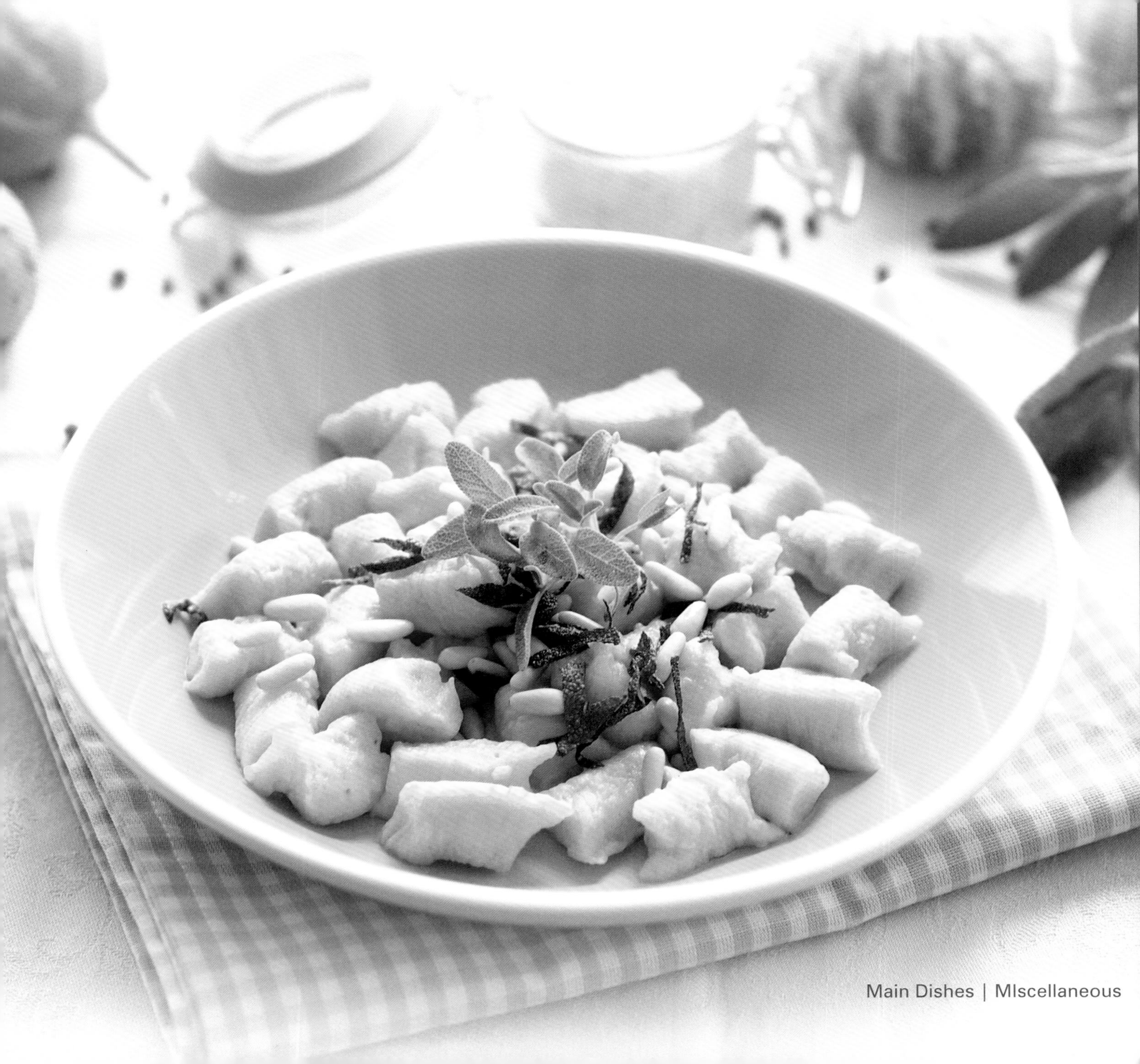

Sweet & Sour Chicken with Vegetables

PREPARATION TIME: 35 min. • **WAITING TIME:** 20 min. • **DIFFICULTY:** Easy

INGREDIENTS

1–1¼ lb	chicken filets
2	spring onions
2	garlic cloves
1	red bell pepper
1	green bell pepper
3 tbsp	coconut oil
3 tbsp	oil
2 tbsp	tomato ketchup
2 tbsp	clary sage vinegar
2 tbsp	sugar
1 tbsp	light soy sauce
½ tsp	salt
1 tsp	sesame oil
½ tbsp	cornstarch
½ C	water

MARINADE

2 tbsp	white wine
2 tbsp	seasoning oil mix (see page 31)
2 tbsp	ginger spice oil (see page 30)
2 tsp	sesame oil
1	chili pepper (or sambal oelek)
1 tbsp	cornstarch

• Cut the chicken filets into cubes. For the marinade, mix the white wine, seasoning oil, ginger spice oil, sesame oil, finely chopped chili pepper (remove seeds) or sambal oelek as well as 1 tbsp of cornstarch. Marinate the chicken for about 20 minutes.
• Meanwhile, finely chop the spring onions (only the white sections) and garlic, and dice the cleaned bell peppers.
• Heat a wok and add 1 tbsp of coconut oil. Add half of the marinated chicken and fry quickly, then remove. Add 1 tbsp of coconut oil and fry the remaining meat and remove it.
• Add remaining oil, then fry spring onions and garlic until the aroma comes out. Add the bell pepper and fry with the rest.

• Mix tomato ketchup, vinegar, sugar, soy sauce, salt, sesame oil, and cornstarch in cup of water, add to the vegetables in the wok and let simmer until it thickens a bit.
• Add the fried chicken and heat through. Serve immediately.

SIDE DISH TIP:
Rice

TIP:
You can use essential garlic oil instead of garlic. Add only at the end and be careful with the amount (no more than 3 drops).

TIP:
If desired, season with more of the seasoning oils.

Side Dishes

All recipes are for 4 portions

Glazed Chestnuts

INGREDIENTS

¼ C	brown sugar
¼ C	water
½ lb	chestnuts, half-cooked*
1 tbsp	cold butter
3–4 drp	orange oil

PREPARATION TIME: 25 min. • **DIFFICULTY:** Medium

• Slowly heat the sugar in a pan until it gets golden and melts, add the water (do not stir!), and leave to boil until the sugar has dissolved completely.
• Warm the chestnuts (microwave oven or hot water bath can be used). Then add the cold butter to the sugar mixture, add the orange oil, and glaze the chestnuts in it.

• Best served as a side dish with red cabbage for various main dishes; excellent for venison.

* You can get commercial peeled and half-cooked chestnuts. Of course, you can boil the chestnuts yourself instead. But you have to calculate a lot more preparation time (for cooking and peeling).

Leek-Apple Cream

INGREDIENTS

2	leeks
1	large sour apple
•	juice of 1 lemon
2 tbsp	butter
1 C	vegetable broth
1 C	crème fraîche
2 drp	cilantroseed oil
1 drp	cardamom oil
1 pinch	sea salt

PREPARATION TIME: 15 min. • **COOKING TIME:** 20 min. • **DIFFICULTY:** Medium

• Thoroughly clean and wash leeks and cut into thin rings (also use the green part of the leek—it is tasty and looks good).
• Peel the apple, cut into cubes, and put into a small bowl; sprinkle with lemon juice so it will not turn brown.
• Heat the butter in a pan and braise the leeks briefly. Add the vegetable soup and let boil until the leeks are soft. Add the apple cubes and briefly braise until they are warm.

• Meanwhile, mix the crème fraîche with the essential oils, remove the pan from the stove, and stir into the leeks and apples. Season with sea salt and serve immediately.

TIP:
You can replace half of the vegetable broth with white wine: deglaze the leek with the white wine and only then add the vegetable broth.

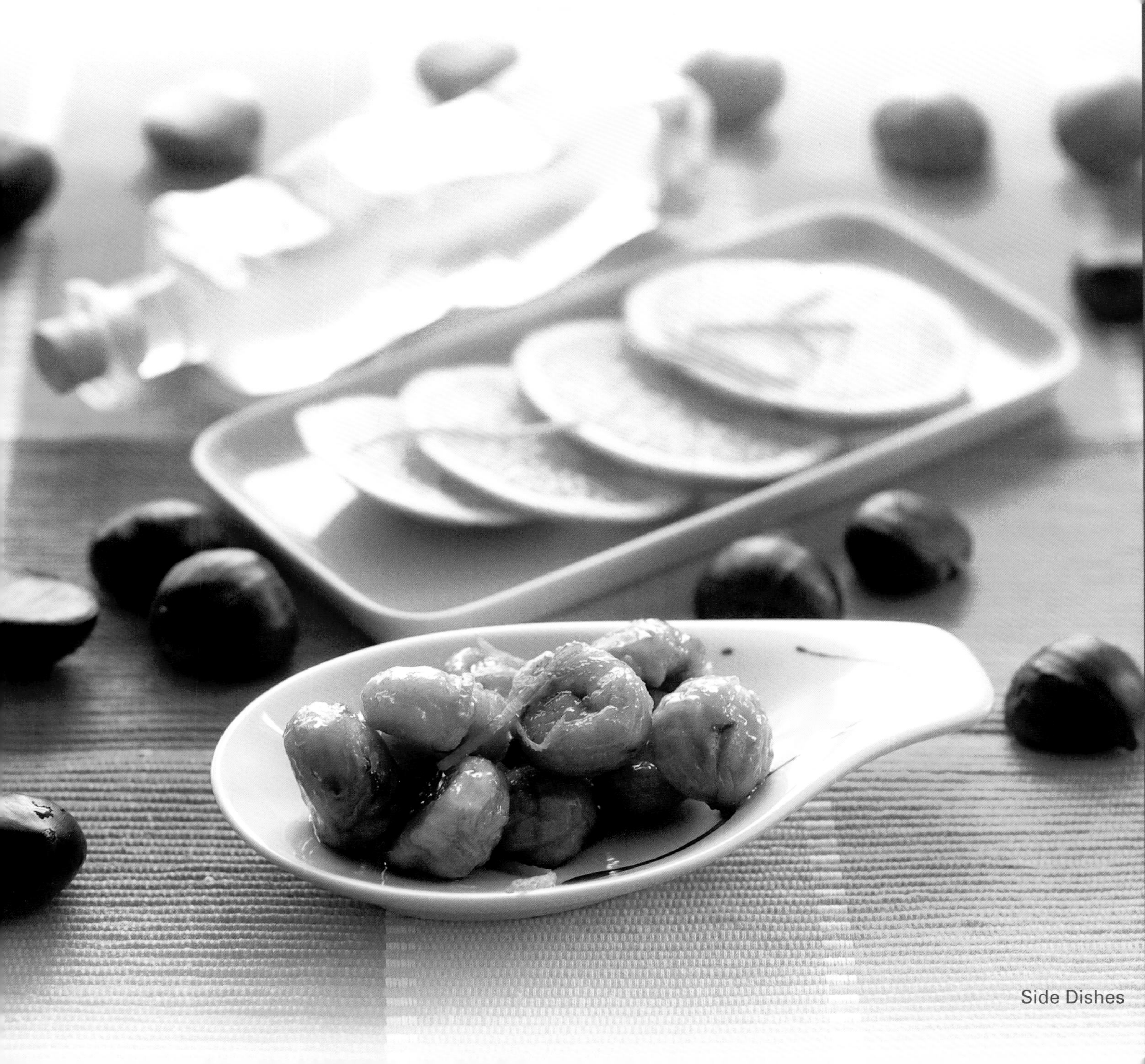

Oriental Carrot Rice

2 cups of rice
½ tsp sea salt
3 carrots
1 tbsp butter
1 tbsp Oriental butter
(see page 34)

PREPARATION TIME: 15 min. • **COOKING TIME:** 20 min. • **DIFFICULTY:** Easy

• Boil 4 cups of water (double the volume of the rice) in a pot and add the rice and the sea salt. Reduce the heat and simmer the rice at low temperature for about 20 minutes until the water has been absorbed by the rice.
• Meanwhile, peel and dice the carrots. Melt the butter in a tall pan and braise the carrots until they are "al dente."

• Once the rice is cooked, mix it with the carrots and season with the Oriental butter.

VARIATION:

Spice the braised carrots with ½ tsp turmeric, and mix into the rice. Emulsify ½ tsp of sea salt with 1–2 drops of cinnamon oil (CO$_2$-extracted). Mix the flavored salt into the carrot rice, and serve immediately.

Red Cabbage with Orange Aroma

INGREDIENTS

1 small head red cabbage
• salt and cumin
• juice of 1 orange
1 onion
2 tbsp olive oil
1 tbsp sugar
½ C red wine
½ apple
1 dash of vinegar
2 drp orange oil

PREPARATION TIME: 20 min. • **COOKING TIME:** Approx. 30 min.
WAITING TIME: Approx. 2 hours • **DIFFICULTY:** Easy

• Clean and finely chop the red cabbage. Add salt and cumin, then marinate in the orange juice for about 1–2 hours.
• Finely chop onion and fry in oil until lightly colored. Add sugar and caramelize, then deglaze the pan with red wine.

• Add the marinated red cabbage and the finely grated apple and braise until soft. Season with a dash of vinegar and 2 drops of orange oil.

Baked Potato
with Flavored Cream

INGREDIENTS   **PREPARATION TIME:** 15 min.   •   **COOKING TIME:** Approx. 45 min.   •   **DIFFICULTY:** Easy

4	large potatoes (mealy, red-skinned variety)
1 C	sour cream
1 pinch	sea salt
1 tbsp	Provençal seasoning oil (see page 31)
4 tbsp	bacon cubes
4 pcs	aluminum foil

• Wrap the potatoes in sufficiently large pieces of aluminum foil and bake in a preheated oven at 350° F, until they are soft (skewer method, see page 122; depending on the size of the potatoes it may take between 30 and 45 minutes).

• Meanwhile, mix the sour cream with the sea salt and the seasoning oil.

• Just before the potatoes are done, fry the bacon cubes without oil in a small pan.

• To serve, cut the top of the aluminum foils in the shape of a star and pull apart; cut the potatoes lengthwise (do not cut through) and pull the halves apart. Put 1 tbsp of flavored sour cream on top and serve with bacon cubes.

TIP:
During springtime you can add fresh, finely chopped wild garlic.

Polenta-Coffee Soufflé

INGREDIENTS

1¾ C water
3½ tbsp butter
1 pinch sea salt
¾ C polenta
  (coarsely ground)
1 pinch ground nutmeg
4 egg yolks
2 drp coffee extract
6 tbsp cream cheese
  (low-fat)
4 egg whites

butter for the baking dishes

PREPARATION TIME: 15 min. • **COOKING TIME:** 50 min. • **DIFFICULTY:** Elaborate

• Boil the water with butter and salt; add polenta and leave to soak for about 20 minutes. Season with ground nutmeg.
• Emulsify the coffee extract with the cream cheese and mix into the soaked polenta.

• Whip the egg whites with a pinch of salt and mix with the polenta.
• Butter 4 individual-size baking dishes and fill with the mixture. Fill a deep dish or a large pan halfway with water. Place the baking dishes into this water bath, and bake in the oven for 30 minutes at 400° F.

Warm Herb Baguette

INGREDIENTS

2 baguettes
¼ lb herb butter
  (recipe on page 33)

PREPARATION TIME: 5 min. • **COOKING TIME:** Approx. 15 min. • **DIFFICULTY:** Easy

• Cut into the baguette with a bread knife every inch or so (do not cut through; the bread loaf should still be hanging together). Put herb butter into these cuts. Bake at 300° F for 15 minutes.

• If you use ready-to-bake baguettes, add herb butter and finish baking in the oven according to the instructions. Serve immediately.

Summer Vegetables with Vanilla and Garlic

INGREDIENTS

2 lb summer vegetables (zucchini, eggplant, garlic, bell pepper, tomatoes)
4 tbsp olive oil
1 drp garlic oil
1 drp vanilla extract

PREPARATION TIME: 30 min. • **DIFFICULTY:** Easy

• Cut vegetables into cubes or slices and fry in 3 tbsp of olive oil. Allow to cool.

• Emulsify the essential oils with 1 tbsp of olive oil and mix with the vegetables.

Red Cabbage with Red Wine and Glühwein Spice

INGREDIENTS

2 lb red cabbage
1 tbsp sugar
1 tsp sea salt
1 apple (optional)
2 C red wine
2-3 tbsp pork lard
5-7 drp Pastries-and-Glühwein oil (a mix of various essential oils)
¼ tsp salt

PREPARATION TIME: 20 min. • **COOKING TIME:** 40–60 min.
WAITING TIME: 24 hours • **DIFFICULTY:** Medium

• Clean the red cabbage and remove the core. Cut finely and marinate in a bowl with the sugar, salt, finely grated apple, and red wine for one day.
• Heat the pork lard in a pot and add the marinated red cabbage. Braise at low temperature until it is tender but not too soft.
• Finish by emulsifying the essential oil mix with ¼ tsp of salt and mixing with the cabbage.

Baby Potatoes with Mint Butter

INGREDIENTS

PREPARATION TIME: 15 min. • **COOKING TIME:** 20–30 min. • **DIFFICULTY:** Easy

20 baby potatoes
(a variety that stays
firm after boiling)
1 tsp sea salt
3 tbsp butter
½ drp peppermint oil

• Peel potatoes and boil in salted water. Drain the potatoes, briefly leave on the stove to steam, then remove from the heat.

• Heat 2 tbsp of butter and add the peppermint oil using the spoon method (see page 21). As soon as it starts to become pearly, add the baby potatoes to the pan and stir with the mint butter.
• Remove from the stove and serve as a side dish for a variety of main dishes.

TIP:
To make sure the potatoes are soft, poke them with a skewer. If the skewer goes in and out easily then they are done. Depending on the size it may take 20 to 30 minutes.

Desserts

All recipes are for 4 portions unless indicated

Apple-Rhubarb Cake with Flavored Meringue

INGREDIENTS

1 C	butter (or coconut oil)
1 C	sugar
2 tbsp	vanilla sugar (see page 38)
2 tbsp	fruit peel sugar (see page 37)
4	eggs
3	egg yolks
1½ C	spelt flour
½ C	cornstarch
4 tsp	baking powder
1 lb	apples
2	rhubarb stems

MERINGUE TOPPING

3	egg whites
1–2 tbsp	orange-bergamot-vanilla honey (see page 37)

butter for the baking dish

PREPARATION TIME: 20 min.　•　**BAKING TIME:** 40 min.　•　**DIFFICULTY:** Medium

• Blend the butter, sugar, vanilla and fruit peel sugar until foamy. One by one, add 4 whole eggs and 3 egg yolks.
• Mix the flour, cornstarch, and baking powder into the dough.
• Spread the dough in a deep, buttered dish. Preheat oven to 400° F.
• Peel and core the apples, and cut into slices. Wash the rhubarb, peel it, and cut the stems into slices. Put them onto the dough and bake for 30 minutes.

• Whip the egg whites until stiff, adding the spice honey just before they are done.
• Remove the cake from the oven after 30 minutes, spread with the flavored egg whites and bake for another 10 minutes, until the meringue is nicely golden. Cool before serving.

Glühwein Pears on Cinnamon Ice Cream

INGREDIENTS

CINNAMON ICE CREAM

1 pint	cream
½ C	milk
1 tsp	cinnamon
6	egg yolks
1¾ C	confectioner's sugar
1 drp	cinnamon bark oil, CO₂-extracted (see page 11)

GLÜHWEIN PEARS

1½ C	Schilcher (Austrian rose wine)
1 C	water
3 C	confectioner's sugar
4 drp	Pastries-and-Glühwein (essential oil mix)
2 drp	thyme oil ct. linalool (see page 62)
4	firm pears

PREPARATION TIME: 40 MIN. • **DIFFICULTY:** Elaborate
FREEZE TIME: 30 min. (ice cream maker) or 5–6 hours (freezer)

• Boil the cream, milk, and cinnamon on medium heat and allow to cool. Meanwhile, whip the egg yolks and the sugar together.
• Add the cooled cream-milk mix and use a whisk to stir over boiling water until you get a thick consistency. Add the cinnamon bark oil, allow to cool, and place into an ice cream maker or the freezer.*
• For the Glühwein pears, boil the wine, water, confectioner's sugar, and half of the essential oils. Add the peeled pears and simmer until the pears are "al dente."
• Remove the pears from the liquid and keep warm. Boil the remaining liquid at high heat into a syrup and flavor with the remaining essential oils.

• Serve the pears with the syrup and the cinnamon ice cream.

If you don't have an ice cream maker, you can freeze by placing the bowl in a freezer for about 5–6 hours. Stir occasionally while freezing.

Fruit Skewers with Orange Sauce

Fruit as desired (e.g., 1 banana, 1 apple, 1 orange, a few grapes)

SAUCE

- juice of 1 orange
- 1 tbsp butter
- 2-3 tbsp brown sugar
- 2 drp orange oil
- 1 drp vanilla extract
- 2 tbsp orange liqueur

PREPARATION TIME: 20 min. • **DIFFICULTY:** Easy

- Peel the fruit if necessary. Cut into small pieces and arrange on wooden skewers.
- Heat the orange juice, butter, and sugar in a pan, stirring until the sugar has dissolved.
- Emulsify the oils with the orange liqueur and add.
- Pour the sauce over the fruit skewers and serve.

Banana Rice with Thyme and Fried Bananas

INGREDIENTS

- 1 C milk
- 2½ tbsp sugar
- 2 large egg yolks
- 4 ripe bananas
- 2 tbsp cane sugar
- 4 drp lemon oil
- 1 drp thyme oil ct. linalool (see page 62)
- 2 drp pepper oil
- 1 bunch of thyme
- some butter for frying

PREPARATION TIME: 30 min. • **DIFFICULTY:** Elaborate
FREEZE TIME: 30 min. (ice cream maker) or 5–6 hours (freezer)

- Heat the milk with the sugar and stir until the sugar has dissolved. Whip the egg yolks until foamy and add to the hot milk mixture, stirring constantly. Place the mixture in a bowl.
- Rinse the milk pot with cold water. Add the egg and milk mixture to it and carefully heat while stirring constantly until it is thick. Remove from the heat and allow to cool.
- Mash 2 bananas with the cane sugar. Add the essential oils and the thyme leaves and pour over the cool egg cream. Place into an ice cream maker or the freezer (see page 126).
- Peel 2 bananas, cut into slices, and fry in butter. Serve with the ice cream.

Spice Soufflé

⅓ C ground almonds
3 tbsp crumbled ginger snaps
1 pinch salt
1 drp each of cinnamon oil, cardamom oil, clove oil, and bay oil
2 drp orange oil
2 tbsp rum
½ orange (untreated), juice and peel
3 tbsp warm butter
4 tsp confectioner's sugar
3 egg yolks
2 oz. chocolate
3 egg whites
1½ tbsp sugar

butter and sugar for the dishes

PREPARATION TIME: 15 min. • **WAITING TIME:** 30 min.
COOKING TIME: Approx. 25 min. • **DIFFICULTY:** Elaborate

• Mix the almonds, crumbled ginger snaps, salt, essential oils, rum, and orange juice and peel. Let sit for about 30 minutes.
• Whip the butter with the confectioner's sugar until foamy, then add the egg yolks one by one and stir. Add the almond-cookie mixture and the finely grated chocolate. Whip the egg whites and sugar and gently mix in.

• Heat the oven to 375° F. Butter 4 individual serving soufflé dishes and sprinkle with sugar. Fill with batter to about one finger below the rim. Fill a large baking dish halfway with hot water; place the dishes into this water bath, and bake for 20–25 minutes.
• Serve with confectioner's sugar sprinkled on top.

Rose Sorbet
with Ylang-Ylang Waffles

INGREDIENTS

SORBET

1 C	rose syrup
2 drp	rose oil
•	juice of 1 orange
2 tbsp	Campari
1 C	Schilcher (Austrian rose wine)
1	egg white

WAFFLES

½ C	soft butter
½ C	sugar
1–2 drp	ylang-ylang oil
2	eggs
1 pinch	salt
1 C	flour
½ tsp	baking powder
1-2 tbsp	whipped cream

PREPARATION TIME: 30 min. • **BAKING TIME:** Approx. 20 min.
WAITING TIME: 2–3 hours • **DIFFICULTY:** Easy

• Mix the rose syrup, rose oil, orange juice, Campari, and wine. Whip the egg white and mix into the liquid. Place into an ice cream maker and leave to freeze.

• Mix all of the ingredients for the waffles with a blender for 2 minutes to prepare a smooth batter, then bake in a waffle iron.

• Serve the warm waffles with the rose sorbet and, if you wish, with sugar-sprinkled rose petals.

TIP:

If you don´t have an ice cream machine, proceed as follows: mix the syrup, rose oil, orange juice, Campari, and wine and put in the freezer. After about 2 hours, mix the stiff egg white into the mixture and freeze for another 30 minutes.

Fruit Salad with Sea-Buckthorn Oil

INGREDIENTS

3	oranges
1	lime
2	bananas
2	apples
½ lb	seasonal fruit (e.g., strawberries, gooseberry, grapes, plums, etc.)
4 tbsp	rum
3–4 drp	orange oil
1 tbsp	sea-buckthorn oil

PREPARATION TIME: 35 min. • **DIFFICULTY:** Easy

• Squeeze 1 orange and 1 lime. Wash the remaining fruit, peel, remove seeds, and cut into cubes or slices. Immediately sprinkle the apples with the orange and lime juice so they don´t turn brown.
• Flavor the rum with the orange oil and pour over the fruit salad, mixing thoroughly.

• Divide the fruit salad into bowls and serve sprinkled with sea-buckthorn oil.

TIP:
Serve garnished with whipped cream.

Tiramisu with Cardamom Coffee

INGREDIENTS

3	cups strong coffee
4	eggs
4 tbsp	brown sugar
1 tbsp	vanilla sugar (see page 38)
2 C	mascarpone
4 tbsp	Grand-Manier
1 drp	cardamom oil
2 drp	coffee extract
1 pkg	ladyfingers
•	cocoa powder for garnishing

PREPARATION TIME: 35 min. • **WAITING TIME:** 3–4 hours • **DIFFICULTY:** Medium

• Brew strong filtered coffee and allow it to cool. Separate the eggs. Whip the egg yolks with the sugar until foamy, and then add the mascarpone.
• Whip the egg whites until stiff and fold into the mascarpone batter. Flavor the Grand Marnier with the cardamom oil and the coffee extract and mix with the coffee.

• Fill a baking dish alternatingly with the lady fingers dipped in the coffee mixture and in the mascarpone batter, finishing with a mascarpone cream layer.
• Sprinkle with cocoa powder and refrigerate for 3–4 hours.

Chocolate Mousse on Raspberry Sauce

INGREDIENTS

½ lb	chocolate (65% cacao)
2½ tbsp	sugar
1 C	whipping cream
4 drp	coffee oil
2 drp	cardamom oil

SAUCE

½ C	sugar
1 C	white wine
½ lb	raspberries (fresh or frozen)
•	chili threads for garnishing

PREPARATION TIME: 15 min. • **WAITING TIME:** Approx. 45 min. • **DIFFICULTY:** Easy

• Melt the chocolate, sugar, and cream over low heat. Add the essential oils and fill into a siphon bottle. Screw a gas cartridge into the top, shake, and put into the fridge.

• Caramelize the sugar for the raspberry sauce, deglaze with white wine, and bring to a boil. Add the raspberries (reserve a few of them) and boil again, then strain through a sieve.

• Use the reserved raspberries to garnish the sauce. Using the siphon bottle, place the chocolate mousse onto plates. Garnish with the raspberry sauce and the chili threads.

TIP:
If you don´t have a siphon bottle, let the cream mixture cool down, blend it with an immersion blender or a mixer. Fill an icing bag with the mousse, and garnish the plates.

Vanilla-Lavender Ice Cream on Cold Berry Soup

1 pint vanilla ice cream
1–2 drp lavender oil

BERRY SOUP

12 oz. berries (currants,
        raspberries,
        blackberries,
        blueberries)
2–3 tbsp sugar
   1 C red grape juice
   2–3 blooming thyme sprigs
   ¼ C Grand Marnier

   1 C whipped cream
   • lavender flowers or
     chocolate crumbles,
     and pirouette cookies
     for garnishing

PREPARATION TIME: 30 min. • **WAITING TIME:** Approx. 4 hours • **DIFFICULTY:** Easy

• Soften the vanilla ice cream enough to mix in the essential lavender oil, then put back into the freezer.
• Wash the berries and let drain. Place them in a pot and mix in the sugar. Cook for 15 minutes over low heat. Add the grape juice and bring to a boil.
• Add lemon thyme sprigs and allow to cool. Add the Grand Marnier when cool and refrigerate for at least 4 hours.
• Pour the berry soup into small ice cream cups and add 1–2 balls of vanilla-lavender ice cream.
• Serve with whipped cream and garnish with lavender flowers or chocolate crumbles, and serve with pirouette cookies.

Rose Frozen Yogurt

INGREDIENTS

¼ C natural yogurt
¼ C rose syrup
5 drp rose oil

PREPARATION TIME: 5 min. • **DIFFICULTY:** Easy
FREEZE TIME: 30 min. (ice cream machine) or 5–6 hours (freezer)

• Mix the ingredients and place into an ice cream maker or the freezer (see page 126).

TIP:
The Ylang-Ylang Waffles on page 130 are perfect to go with this dish.

Panna Cotta with Tonka Bean-Vanilla Aroma

INGREDIENTS

2 C whipping cream
5 tsp vanilla sugar
4 tbsp granulated sugar
3 leaves of gelatin
1 drp vanilla extract
2 drp tonka bean oil
(or 4 drops orange oil)

PREPARATION TIME: 30 min. • **WAITING TIME:** 1–2 hours • **DIFFICULTY:** Easy

• Boil the cream with the sugar and leave on low heat for about 10 minutes. Soak the gelatin in cold water, squeeze well, and dissolve in the warm cream-sugar mix.

• Flavor with the vanilla extract and tonka bean oil (or orange oil). Refrigerate until it becomes firm, then serve with fruit.

TIP:
Panna Cotta is easy to prepare ahead of time!

Vanilla Ice Cream with Bergamot Aroma on Strawberry Puree

INGREDIENTS

2 C vanilla ice cream
2 tbsp orange-bergamot-vanilla honey (see page 37)
½ C strawberries
1 tbsp dandelion or maple syrup
1 C whipped cream
• chocolate crumbles and pirouette cookies for garnishing

PREPARATION TIME: 25 min. • **FREEZE TIME:** 1–2 hours • **DIFFICULTY:** Easy

• Soften the vanilla ice cream slightly and add the spice honey to it using a blender; put back in the freezer.
• Wash strawberries and let them drain. Mash with an immersion blender and sweeten with the dandelion or maple syrup.

• Place the flavored strawberry puree on dessert plates and put 1–2 vanilla ice cream balls on top. Serve with whipped cream, chocolate crumbs, and pirouette cookies..

Drinks

The following recipes are mostly for larger quantities

Apple Punch

INGREDIENTS

1½ qt	apple juice
1½ qt	water
1	cinnamon stick
1	orange (untreated)
1 drp	ginger oil, CO_2-extracted
1 drp	cinnamon bark oil, CO_2-extracted (see page 11)
2–3 drp	blood orange oil
1–2 tbsp	honey (or brown sugar)

PREPARATION TIME: 15 min.
DIFFICULTY: Easy

• Slowly heat apple juice and water in a pot and add the cinnamon stick and the orange cut into slices.
• Emulsify the essential oils with the honey or sugar and blend.
• Serve hot, garnished with orange or lemon slices.

Flavored Tea

INGREDIENTS

11 oz	dry black tea
3 drp	fruit peel mix oil
1 drp	cinnamon oil, CO_2-extracted (see page 11)
1 drp	ginger oil, CO_2-extracted (see page 11)
1 drp	cardamom oil (spoon method; see page 21)
1 drp	cocoa extract

PREPARATON TIME: 5 min.
WAITING TIME: 2–3 weeks
DIFFICULTY: Easy

• Mix the dry black tea with the essential oils and put into a dark screw-top jar. Leave for 2–3 weeks, shaking occasionally.
• Prepare tea as usual.

Glühwein

INGREDIENTS

1 qt	good red wine
½ qt	water
1	cinnamon stick
1	orange (untreated)
15 drp	Pastry & Glühwein oil (mix of several essential oils)
4 tbsp	brown sugar

PREPARATION TIME: 15 min.
DIFFICULTY: Easy

• Slowly heat the red wine and the water with the cinnamon stick in a pot.
• Add the orange, cut into slices.
• Emulsify the Pastry & Glühwein oil with the sugar and add to the red wine. Serve hot.

Lilac Syrup

INGREDIENTS

2 qt	water
10 C	sugar
3	lemon slices (untreated)
3–4	panicles of lilac blossoms
2 oz.	fresh lemon juice
1 tsp	sugar
3 drp	grapefruit oil

PREPARATION TIME: 45 min.
WAITING TIME: 3–4 days
DIFFICULTY: Easy

• Boil water with sugar and lemon slices and let cool. Pluck the lilac blossoms from the panicles and add with the lemon juice into the syrup.
• Leave covered in a cool place for 3–4 days.
• Mix 1 tsp sugar with the grapefruit oil (acts as a conserving agent) and add.
• Strain the syrup and pour into clean bottles. Store in a cool place.

Lavender Syrup

INGREDIENTS

4 lb	sugar
3 qt	water
2½ oz	lavender flowers
3	lemon slices (untreated)
6 tbsp	lavender hydrolate or 1–2 drp lavender oil
2 oz	fresh lemon juice

PREPARATION TIME: 15 min.
WAITING TIME: 5–6 days
DIFFICULTY: Easy

• Boil the sugar and water and let cool.
• Add the lavender blooms with the lemon slices. Add the lavender oil or lavender hydrolate emulsified with the lemon juice and leave for 5–6 days in an earthenware pot in a cool place.
• Strain the syrup and pour into bottles.

Rose Syrup

INGREDIENTS

1½ C	sugar
1 C	water
1 tbsp	lemon juice
3 tbsp	rose hydrolate or ½ drp rose oil (spoon method; see page 21)

PREPARATION TIME: 15 min.
DIFFICULTY: Easy

• Boil the sugar and water with the lemon juice in a pot, stirring constantly.
• Leave to simmer at low heat until the syrup coats the back of the spoon.
• Remove from the heat, let cool and mix in the rose flower hydrolate or the rose oil. Pour into clean bottles.

TIP:
The syrup can be kept in the fridge for several weeks.

TIP:
If you dilute these syrups with water or mineral water you get wonderful refreshing drinks. If you use them without dilution they are great for flavoring ice cream or for cocktails with sparkling wines or champagne.

The Right Menu

for almost any occasion

It can be a lot of fun to prepare a tasty menu for the right occasion and to enjoy it with your guests. But there are many who are wary of putting a several-course meal on the table. Sometimes our best intentions end in disaster due to insufficient preparation.

In this chapter we want to help you by providing the right tips for the preparation and realization of a successful evening, where you can share the meal with your guests in a relaxed way.

Tips and Tricks

More than anything, cooking means "good organization." You can be as creative and skillful as the best chefs, but if you don't organize your dinner menu with enough forethought you might get into trouble.

First, consider the following questions:
• How many guests are to be invited?
• Who are these guests? Do they have particular preferences or dislikes with respect to food (vegetarians, no alcohol, dislike particular foods, are not allowed to eat certain ingredients, etc.)?
• What kind of theme are you planning for the evening? This not only has an influence on the menu but also on the garnishing and the choice of drinks.

If you know what you are aiming for, you are ready to plan the menu.

Generally, when putting together menus, be careful to sequence the food to avoid repetition in the dishes:
• The same product (e.g., meat, poultry). Fish can appear several times—however, it needs to different kinds of fish.
• The same method of preparation (e.g., grilled, baked, stuffed).
• The same color (such as tomato soup and spaghetti with red sauce).
• The same soup ingredients and side dishes (e.g., marrow dumpling soup and potato dumplings).

Menus for Special Occasions

You can find the dishes indicated in the menu suggestions in the recipe section (page 48–138). The page number of each recipe is given.

Each menu features useful information, required steps for the preparation, and special tips for the particular menu.

As you prepare, keep the following things in mind:
• Menu sequence
• Allow sufficient time for purchasing the ingredients for the menu. Nothing is worse than realizing on the day of the event that you missed something and might not be able to get it.
• Many dishes can be largely prepared the day before the event. This saves a lot of time and stress, and makes it possible for you to enjoy the meal with your guests.

Light Summer Menu

Tomato and Avocado Carpaccio
(page 50)

**Indian Meatballs
with Aromatic Sauce**
(page 66)

**Lemon-Garlic Char with
Herb Baguette and Leaf Salad**
(pages 97, 118, 51)

Fruit Skewers with Orange Sauce
(page 127)

TIPS:
You can prepare the meatballs and the sauce the day before. The sour cream and spices must be blended spices early so the flavors are absorbed. Before serving, put the meatballs in a 200° F oven for a few minutes.

You can make the herb baguette several days before and freeze it. Heat it in the oven before serving.

Menu for a Romantic Evening

**Vegetable Skewers
with Rose Marinade**
(page 60)

Indian Tomato Soup
(page 76)

**Coquilles St.-Jacobs
with Sliced Vegetables**
(page 96)

**Vanilla Ice Cream
with Bergamot Aroma
on Strawberry Puree**
(page 138)

TIPS:
You can prepare the vegetable skewers several hours before and keep them in a cool place. Season some 30 minutes before with the marinade. Spray the rose hydrolate on just before serving.

The Indian tomato soup can be prepared the day before. You only need to heat it up and serve with fresh peppermint.

Prepare the vegetable slices for the Coquilles St.-James a few hours ahead. The dish itself must be prepared just before serving.

The flavored vanilla ice cream and the strawberry puree can also be prepared the day before. You only need to serve it.

Party Buffet

Pumpkin Soup and Warm Herb Baguette
(pages 74, 118)

**Avocado Salad with Shrimp and
Lime Oil Dressing**
(page 48)

**Buffet with Various Spreads & Salads
with Different Kinds of Bread**
(pages 50–58)

**Apple-Rhubarb Cake
with Flavored Meringue**
(page 124)

TIPS:

*You can prepare the pumpkin soup the day before or a
few hours ahead of time. Heat before serving. Mix the
crème fraîche with the essential oils, and whisk together
with an immersion blender.*

*The avocado-shrimp salad should rest for at least 4
hours. You can prepare it the day before. The spreads
should also rest overnight. Prepare the day before and
keep in the fridge.*

Bake the rhubarb cake a few hours before the feast.

For Important Guests

Orange Dates with Bacon
(page 64)

Riesling Soup with Cinnamon Oil
(page 75)

**Beef Medallions with Orange-Pepper Sauce
and Pumpkin Gnocchi**
(pages 87, 108)

Tiramisu with Cardamom Coffee
(page 132)

TIPS:

*You can prepare the orange dates a few hours ahead of time
and then heat them for a few minutes in a 200° F oven.*

*You may prepare the Riesling soup the day before. Heat before
serving. Mix the crème fraîche with the essential oils, and whip
foamy together the immersion blender.*

*Pumpkin gnocchi can be prepared for storage and frozen
when half-cooked. Finish cooking in hot water just before
serving and finish as indicated in the recipe.*

*The cardamom tiramisu should rest overnight. You can
prepare it the day before and keep it cool in the fridge.*

Magic Christmas Menu

Strudel Dough Baskets with Mushroom Filling
(page 62)

**Cauliflower Soup
with Coconut Milk and Ginger Oil**
(page 79)

**"Aristo" Pork Filet
with Polenta-Coffee Soufflé**
(pages 84, 118)

Glühwein Pears on Cinnamon Ice Cream
(page 126)

TIPS:

You can prepare the strudel dough baskets a few hours before serving. Put the mushroom filling into the baskets just before serving.

The cauliflower soup can also be prepared the day before. Store in a cool place, heat before serving, and finish as indicated in the recipe.

You can lard the pork filet with the cloves and the garlic the evening before. Season and leave to rest in the fridge overnight.

Prepare the cinnamon ice cream and the glühwein pears the day before. Briefly warm up the pears before serving.

Vegan Menu

Leaf Salad with Orange Vinaigrette
(page 51)

**Zucchini Cream Soup
with Lemongrass Oil
and Roasted Pinenuts**
(page 82)

**Savoy Cabbage Rolls
with Boiled Potatoes**
(page 106)

Fruit Salad with Sea-Buckthorn Oil
(page 132)

TIPS:

You can prepare the zucchini-lemongrass soup the day before. Store in a cool place, warm before serving, and sprinkle with toasted pinenuts (toasted the day before).

The rolls can be prepared a few hours ahead of time. Finish according to the recipe just before serving. At the same time, prepare the boiled potatoes.

Prepare the fruit salad a few hours ahead of time and leave covered in a cool place. Add fresh lemon juice so the fruit doesn´t turn brown.

Vegetarian Menu

**Arugula Salad with Lemon
Vinaigrette**
(page 52)

Carrot Soup with Lime Oil
(page 70)

Rose Pasta with Rose-Mint Pesto
(page 105)

**Vanilla-Lavender Ice Cream on
Cold Berry Soup**
(page 136)

TIPS:

You can prepare the carrot soup the day before. Heat before serving and finish according to the recipe.

The lavender ice cream and the cold berry soup can be prepared the day before and kept cool in the fridge or the freezer.

Alphabetical Recipe Index

The Authors

The authors consider cooking and good food to be creative and enjoyable. From this creativity sprang forth the idea to use essential oils in the preparation of dishes. This is how the *aroma kitchen* came to be: cooking with essential oils means there are unimagined culinary sensations and the highest level of enjoyment to be experienced.

Sabine Hönig

Born in Frankfurt am Main, Germany, Hönig has been active as a corporate counselor, coach, and trainer since 1999. The focus of her work lies in the areas of personal development, stress management, and burn-out prevention, as well as in health and wellness areas. As a licensed aroma therapist she combines classic counseling, coaching, and training in her everyday work. This combination has proven to be very effective in combatting stress, preventing burnout, and loosening energetic-mental blocks. The essential oils assist in forming a bridge between the emontional and the mental-logic levels of her customers. It is quite simple and easy to discover unexpected resources and to deal with issues on entirely new levels.

Hönig inherited her love for cooking and the appreciation of delicious dishes in the intimacy of the family from her parents. "At our home it was always important to enjoy meals together as a family. We had a large vegetable garden and fresh herbs, and we always fed one of the pigs per year on our neighbor´s farm. Even when my sister and I were still children we used to participate in the preparation of fruits, vegetables, and meat. This is how we never lost the connection to our food."

Sabine Hönig is married and lives in Graz, Austria.

Web: www.meta-sense.at | E-mail: sabine.hoenig@meta-sense.at

Ursula Kutschera

Kutschera is a licensed aroma therapy practitioner and a licensed herbalist, and worked at a large Austrian bank until 2007. During this period her curiosity about essential oils and their influence on the human being came to light. So her path towards becoming a licensed aroma therapy practitioner was laid out. She has been involved in elaborate aroma counseling sessions, bodywork with essential oils, and concepts regarding the aromatization of rooms, as well as in giving conferences and workshops about essential oils and natural cooking with essential oils. Natural healing, herbs, and their effects have accompanied Kutschera since childhood. Her grandmother piqued her interest in herbs and the old knowledge about them. For years, this passionate cook has used essential oils to prepare dishes and creates new recipes. Her daughter, who shares her passion for cooking, thinks that using essential oils is simply fantastic, especially when fresh spices and herbs are not available. Kutschera shares her knowledge about the aroma kitchen by giving cooking classes dedicated to essential oils.

Kutschera is married with two adult children and lives in Graz, Austria.

Web: www.aroma-garten.at | E-Mail: ursula.kutschera@aon.at